The Forgotten War

Texas Veterans Remember Korea

Mackey Murdock

Republic of Texas Press
Plano, Texas

Library of Congress Cataloging-in-Publication Data

Murdock, Mackey.
   The forgotten war: Texas veterans remember Korea / Mackey Murdock.
      p.   cm.
   Includes bibliographical references and index.
   ISBN 1-55622-899-6
   1. Korean War, 1950-1953–Personal narratives, American. 2. Veterans—United
States—Biography. 3. Murdock, Mackey. I. Title.

DS921.6 M87 2002
951.904'28—dc21   2002000461

951.90428
M974

Republic of Texas Press is an imprint of Wordware Publishing, Inc.
No part of this book may be reproduced in any form or by
any means without permission in writing from
Wordware Publishing, Inc.

Printed in the United States of America

ISBN 1-55622-899-6
10 9 8 7 6 5 4 3 2 1
0203

All inquiries for volume purchases of this book should be addressed to
Wordware Publishing, Inc., at 2320 Los Rios Boulevard, Plano, Texas 75074.
Telephone inquiries may be made by calling:

(972) 423-0090

Contents

Contents

To my wife, Joanne, my daughters, Sheri and Julie, and my grandson Shane—the family I asked for and with which I have been blessed.

Preface

In 1950 the word war had a dirty ring. Reminding the electorate of the recent unpleasantness that had consumed the first half of the prior decade was politically unwise. Just after the hottest of all conflicts and a few years before the Cuban Missile Crisis put the deep freeze on the Cold War, the world had fought enough. United Nations and Washington policy-makers found "police action" a more appealing term and so dubbed their mission on Korea's stretch of refuse. If it qualified as a police beat, it became the bloodiest.

Politicians welcomed the birth of spin almost fifty years before the public did. The news media and politically correct government officials adopted "police action" as appropriate. The Americans that fought it knew better. Fifty-four thousand failed to live through it.

Make no mistake, it was war at its worst and most who manned the beat were nonpolitical. Few thought of social correctness, and nearly all had yet to vote. The era of patriotism lived, heroes died. Individual countries of the United Nations mustered their young. Seasoned veterans, soft peacetime militia, and expendable civilians answered the call. These young people received few options and, upon receiving their pay, realized their paper worth to be less than a hundred dollars a month. Ten thousand dollars of government-paid life insurance cleared the books in the event of death.

Still, in a day when causes lived, they became as efficient, as honorable a fighting force as ever manned the line. Their futures were put on hold. They fought for their buddies and killed to live.

Then the lucky ones came home, generally to grateful and loving families. Too modest to recognize public indifference, many soothed lonely nights with brew made tasteless by memories of war too horrible to acknowledge. Being alive brought a certain degree of guilt.

This land, which America's young men found so repulsive, strange, and easy to hate, today warrants the title hallowed ground. Purified by time, washed by fluids of the dead and dying, and sanctified by suffering and death along its battered ridges and flat paddies, its memories beckon the veteran back. Horrible incidents like the death of a friend, the suffering of a wound near a small hamlet, surrender near an out-of-the-way village, gave it significance and requires, in hindsight, the accuracy of dates and the proper spelling of foreign sounding names.

Aging servicemen from all nations that fought there revisit the scene. Often they view it through misty eyes. They recognize that foot after foot of what they once deemed odorous soil is in fact the precious cover that entombs the death of innocence.

The following is a sampling of experiences from those gallant men: your loved ones, perhaps a father, husband, brother, or sweetheart, definitely my buddies with whom so many share a bond and all owe a debt. Here are the stories most people never hear—the ones seldom discussed, except among those who lived them.

Third-Time Charm

The night of September 2, 1951 lay warm and humid over Denton, Texas. In those days drugstores and theatres sported air conditioning. Most residences did not. My bus route from West Texas to the Dallas Naval Receiving Station had brought me there. A chance for a free bunk and a little BS with Bill Ratliff provided the incentive to lay over.

I'd catch the bus into Dallas early the next morning to be on schedule reporting for active duty. There was a lot of stuff happening in a place called Korea. I didn't know much about it, but after thirteen years, schoolrooms were becoming confining.

Ratliff and I had shared an old fraternity house with about twenty other guys the previous spring. Now between semesters, everyone but Bill had gone home for a week. Being tied to a part-time job in a shoe store kept him fighting loneliness in Denton and between semesters, manning the deserted Falcon fraternity house. Older, and a veteran of the World War II's naval battle of Midway, he was ready for company. We had a few beers and hit the sack sometime around midnight.

Pain from frying nerve endings in my left wrist woke me sometime later. Things were confused. The night that started warm had turned into a furnace. I slapped at my left arm and realized my bedding was on fire. Brilliant flames leapt about the ancient, papered walls and contrasted with outside darkness. My ears roared with the sound of out of control flames and a pounding heart. Reasoning floundered. Panic prevailed. I sensed being upright, perhaps standing in bed, perhaps on the floor. I threw myself toward the doorway that opened to the hall. Once through that door, it was only a couple of steps to the stairway.

Fire encircled the door and snaked out in hungry, licking motions. The heat blinded and the smoke choked, but a shadow offered a chance there between the flames. Unaware that the door stood half ajar, I straddled then slammed into it. Pain in my forehead and nose joined that in my arm and I fell, dazed.

My first memory from the floor was of watching the hallway and stairwell outside the door exploding in flames. Later I realized that running into that partially opened door had saved my life, but at the moment I gathered myself, thinking rationally for the first time since awakening. There was less smoke near the floor, and I thought of the open window at the foot of my bed. It opened to the roof of the building.

"Murdock. Swede. Swede, where are you?" Ratliff's voice came from somewhere beyond the flames. How'd he get out of that room?

I knocked the flimsy screen from the window and stepped barefoot onto the two-foot wide, composition shingles and into fresh air. Flame licked at my boxer shorts as I moved from the window. I crept carefully along the high roof and toward the porch and a chance to get to a lower eave.

A moment later I sat on the edge of the porch roof and contemplated rolling over and lowering myself at arm's length before dropping. Angled bricks formed a flowerbed border directly beneath the drip line. Still, jumping beyond it meant a pretty forceful leap. Large windows behind me exploded outward from the buildup of heat, and broken glass filled the air around me.

There's no memory of the decision. I pushed off and outward and flew through the flame-lit darkness. My last thought was, so what, a piece of cake. The landing brought home not only my frailty, but also the realization that even nineteen-year-olds are mortal. Something happened in my ankle that made me forget the burned, sticky flesh on my arm. A moan escaped my throat.

"Murdock! Murdock, where are you?" Bill's voice tore through my senses, bouncing back and forth against that wall of heat and flame. So far as he knew, I was still in the bedroom upstairs.

"Bill, down here. Oh, hell! Uuumh, I'm out here in the yard," I yelled.

Bill was at my side in an instant. "Shit! Man, I thought you were gone. Where you hurt?"

"How'd you get out of there?"

"Got hot and moved downstairs before I ever went to sleep. Where you hurt?"

A police car arrived, lights flashing. I may have answered Bill. I may not. At that moment it occurred to me that I was nude except for shorts. The streets filled with excited people. The officer and Bill helped me hobble to the backseat of a squad car.

Flow Memorial Hospital doctors X-rayed the leg and diagnosed the problem as a simple fracture of the right tibia that extended into the ankle joint. Before noon, a chief petty officer from the Dallas Naval Recruiting Office knocked on my hospital room door.

He introduced himself. "You're U.S. Naval Reserve Recruit Mackey Murdock."

"Yes, sir."

"We got a phone message from the nurse's desk. Looks like you've had a busy night, Recruit Murdock."

"Busy enough, sir."

"Well, I went by the house on Oak Street. There's not much left over there. Then I went down and checked with the fire department. They listed the cause of the fire as bad wiring. Did you know?"

"No, sir."

"Yes, well they did. Mr. Murdock, it looks like you are going to remain a civilian for a while. You'll continue your reserve training at Dallas' weekly meetings as soon as you're able to get around. Okay?"

"Does that mean I'm not on active duty after all, sir?"

"That's the way it looks, son. You came close, but, as of now, you're still a civilian. Any questions?"

"No, sir. Thank you, sir."

"Good luck, young man."

The chief's analysis was overturned then confirmed a number of times during the next two weeks, each time by higher-ranking brass. Finally, three weeks later and after I'd enrolled in then cancelled back out of college, each time based on the navy's latest input, a captain from the 8th Naval District Headquarters in New Orleans called my hometown. Somehow, we made connection at the telephone office.

"Recruit Murdock," the voice on the telephone said, "this is Captain ____, 8th Naval District, New Orleans. Seems we've been bouncing you around a bit, lad. What's your status now? Are you enrolled back in college or not?"

"No sir, I cancelled my registration yesterday based on the navy's latest phone call."

There was a long pause. "Murdock, the confusion has stemmed around whether or not you were on active duty at the time of your accident. Officially you were. You had left your home and were en route to report to Dallas Naval Receiving."

How many versions of that story had I heard in the last three weeks? I leaned against the narrow wall at the top of a flight of stairs. I held the phone's receiver in one hand and both crutches in the other. Narrow stairs led to the street below. The phone, housed in oak with two large owl-like eyes above the snout of a mouthpiece, had a separate receiver. The whole thing was mounted on the exterior wall of the phone office.

The captain cleared his throat. "We are going to leave it up to you. You can either remain a civilian and take care of your own medical bills then report for active duty in six months or we'll have a hospital plane pick you up tomorrow at Shepperd Air Force Base in Wichita Falls. In that case your active duty status will be effective retroactive to the original date you left home to report. Of course we'll reimburse all of your medical expenses. You'll go on to further duty after your recuperation."

There it was again, another chance to volunteer. How many had it been now? First was joining the reserves, then active duty as soon as I became eligible. Now this made three. I weighed the decision a few seconds. It became more difficult each time.

Since the original option I'd met a girl, seen a little of boot camp, and after a broken leg, realized I could be hurt. A pact with Carl Kisinger and Bill Mackey loomed big in the background. We'd all agreed we were dropping out of school and going into the service. They were gone. Now it was my turn. So far as the girl was concerned, leaving for college a couple of years earlier had taught me that the hometown ladies kept memories of me about as long as it took for my dust to settle when I reached the state highway.

"What'll it be, son?"

"Consider me in the navy, sir. How will I know what time to catch that plane?"

"We'll send you a telegram tonight. Welcome aboard, sailor."

"Thank you, sir.... Sir, it's my sea bag. It and all my uniforms, all my gear, burned up in that fire. And, sir, where am I going?"

"Don't worry, you are going to Corpus Christi, we'll take care of everything down there. Good luck."

I took a deep breath and looked down the steep stairwell to the open wooden door at street level. Dust swirled in its opening while more drifted past and moved on down the high sidewalk of my hometown. I took a deep breath and somehow felt a little older than my nineteen years. I clunked awkwardly but carefully down the stairs. One more night, I thought.

Backdoor to War

The following evening I leaned back in my seat listening to the sounds of flight and the steady drone of a hospital plane's engines. The C-46 banked, bringing into view the street and harbor lights that outlined the horseshoe shape of Corpus Christi Bay.

I'd discovered upon boarding at Wichita Falls that the crew consisted of two pilots and a crisply starched air force nurse. A serviceman in pajama bottoms and wearing a straightjacket and I made up the passenger list. His dog tags labeled him as military, but I had no idea of what branch. He had a way of staring through you. I'd made the mistake of making eye contact with him when I first boarded. I avoided it the balance of the flight. In addition to the confinement of his jacket, he was snuggly strapped to a bunk that hung alongside empty ones on the starboard side of the plane.

I'd deliberately dropped that starboard navy term for right on the nurse earlier. She and I shared a bench seat across the aisle from the restrained guy. Having used half of the navy vocabulary I'd retained from July's two-week reserve boot training in San Diego, I had reservations about the temptation of exhausting my repertoire by dropping the word port on the young lady.

I decided against it. I sensed she realized I was about as salty as rainwater. The lady looked like she'd been around. Still, until that plane landed her choices were limited. They boiled down to the mental patient or me. I'd learned early on to look for the bright side. I'd not, unfortunately, learned how to make idle chatter. After five hundred miles of trying to talk to a lock-jawed country boy, I got the feeling the patient across the aisle was looking better to her, hence my interest in the harbor lights.

Minutes later a seaman drove a navy stenciled van onto the runway and parked near the plane. He helped me aboard. Two corpsmen gathered up the mental patient and carried him off in an ambulance. The nurse gave me a sisterly smile and wished me good luck. I didn't see her leave the plane. The sailor drove through the base and toward the entrance of Ward 111 of the Naval Air Station Hospital. The smell of the sea enveloped the base, and the van's lights illuminated white buildings and palm trees.

The driver parked then helped me to the door. He pointed, "In there check in at the nurse's desk."

Normally inductees into the military enter their tour through the doors of basic or boot training—the front door. Most emerge toughened, pissed-off, and anxious to encounter the enemy. In the words of some, they feel nine feet tall and bulletproof. It's later, after watching the death and suffering of others or struggling with the pain of their own wounds, they begin to understand that the backdoor to war is crowded with the wounded and the dying. Little did I know I was about to cross that rear threshold.

I struggled with my crutches, fumbling with my telegram and a small bag. I backed, butt-first, through the screen door then turned. Two wheelchairs raced past; one swerved to avoid hitting me. "Look out!" A voice shouted.

I staggered back and bounced against the wall. A kid maybe eighteen years old grabbed one of his chair's wheels. It slid into a swerving arch and he and his racer came to a stop. This fellow might weigh a hundred and twenty pounds after a large meal and toting a sea bag.

"You okay?" he asked then continued before I could answer. "Didn't mean to run you down. That damn Hall takes up the whole aisle with them long arms." The kid turned both wheels and pulled up beside me. He stopped and stuck out his hand. "Name's Pruitt. Looks like you're just coming in."

"Mackey Murdock, nice to meet you." I looked at Hall who sat watching from twenty feet away. One footrest on his chair was raised and his long right leg extended straight ahead of the chair. It rested on a pillow. I nodded.

He smiled and hooked a finger at the nurse's glassed-in cubicle. "She'll take care of you."

At the cubicle I stammered my name and then handed the nurse, a lieutenant, the telegram. "I broke my leg getting out of a fire," I explained. I could hear Pruitt and Hall bantering back and forth in the connecting hallway to our left.

The nurse called a corpsman and pointed. "Give Mackey number eight. He's a navy recruit, hurt in transit to active duty. He'll need pajamas. We'll let the yeoman figure out what's going on with him tomorrow. Show him around."

The corpsman walked me to my bed, showed me where to store my personal items, then sat in a chair nearby while I put my things away. "See you met Bobby Don and Pruitt," he said.

"Bobby Don must be the big guy."

"Yeah, come on, I'll show you the head."

Bobby Don Hall

The hospital formed a series of H's with the horizontal crossbar formed by a connecting hallway. Each ward formed a vertical leg of the H and was identified by a number. The nurses' offices sat midway of each ward at the connecting hall. The building, one story and wood frame, had narrow windows placed inches apart along its length. Along each wall, beds were spaced, head to the wall, with room for a chair between. A twelve-foot space separated the feet of the bunks to form an aisle in each ward. There were at least five wards.

Later Pruitt came and sat on the bunk beside me. We talked until lights-out. We shared hometown locations and I learned he was from Fort Worth and a marine PFC. At that time I still measured the men I met somewhat by physical stature. A bit miffed at his nearly running me down, I had this pint-sized marine earmarked as just another kid. Someone I could take in a minute, broken leg or no. Getting to know Pruitt took that childish standard out of mind forever. He wore no outward sign of injury.

"What are you in here for?" I asked.

"My stomach."

"What's wrong with your stomach?"

"They removed a good portion of my intestines." Pruitt lit a cigarette. His manner was matter of fact, almost disinterested.

"How come they did that?"

"Korea, a Chinese burp-gun got me." His eyes flickered, just once, then he lifted his head, and his gaze followed the upward spiraling smoke from his cigarette. Somber now, the exuberance of youth on his face was replaced with a void of nothingness as blank as sky's eons of darkness.

I felt stupid, childish. "I'm sorry, I didn't mean to get personal."

"No, it's okay, I'll tell you about it one of these days. That's what we do best around here, swap war stories. How'd you hurt your leg?"

"There was a house fire. I had to bail out. It's nothing, just a simple break."

Pruitt may have sensed my embarrassment. "Hall over there took a bullet through that kneecap," he said.

The overhead lights went off, but soft nightlights provided visibility about the ward. Pruitt bade me goodnight and went to his bunk. For the next couple of hours, men drifted in out of the night, returning from liberty. I lay in my bunk listening to the tap of their walking canes or the softer scrape of crutches on the tile floor as they made their way down the semi-darkened ward. The windows were open to the failing sea breeze and the moon cast shadows of racing clouds.

Sleep eluded me. I thought of Carl Kisinger at sea somewhere in the Pacific aboard a carrier, the USS *Essex*. Bill Mackey came to mind. The last I'd heard, he was aboard the Destroyer Escort 442—the USS *Ulvert M. Moore*.

Memory returned of the three of us agreeing we'd drop out of school and volunteer for the service. This thing is for real, I thought, and I'm stuck with it for the next two years. Talk about crazy, we must have been bored to death. You'd think I'd learn after a while that forming community agreements, gang pacts, was kid stuff.

First there been the time when, at eight years of age, two cousins and I and an older uncle slipped out into the night and built a fire. Sitting by the ditch where we normally caught tadpoles, we whispered our way through the rituals we'd formed for our night council of the Brotherhood of Girl Haters.

We slashed small crosses with a penknife on our fingertips and swore a blood oath to never kiss, hold hands with, or even sit next to a girl. After pondering some time for a proper penalty, something short of death, for anyone who violated our pact, we decided upon a two-mile trail of tears, barefoot through stickers. In addition to being without shoes, the guilty member would be clad with only undershorts stuffed with sandpaper or burrs in the most vulnerable areas of wear. That agreement had been harmless enough. It'd died an orphan's death.

My second encounter with pacts occurred in high school when two friends and I drew straws to see who would challenge the local bully to a fistfight. The lighter of the three drew the shortest straw and, true to form, I volunteered to take his place and be first to challenge the older boy. The idea was that if the first of our group got whipped then the second member of this band of idiots would try the guy the following week. Surely one of the three of us could whip him.

Loyal to my duty, I called the guy out the following week. Actually, I was watching a movie when these great friends all came in and said, "He's out there; you've been looking for him."

I flagged the older boy over on Main Street. "You've bullied your way around here long enough," I said. "Get out of that pickup. I'm gonna whip your ass."

Seeing he had no chance of saving face, he followed me to the nearby shadows. It was just the two of us. He tried to change my mind by pulling a knife. Failing to deter me from my mission of honor and knighthood, he licked the dickens out of me. After seeing my face the next day, the other boys decided the bully was really a nice guy after all, and we all continued our days of high school bliss.

You'd have thought I'd learn from the experience. But no, three years later, finding injustice still existed in the world, I entered into this last agreement with the two college buddies, Bill Mackey and Carl Kisinger. Some bad news was coming out of a place called Korea. A police action over there caused our high school chums, not now in college, to be drafted. From the looks of my current companions, the consequences of that act had all the earmarks of my having entered a meat grinder of a magnitude I'd never dreamed.

From the other end of the darkened room pain-filled sounds of a hurting patient pleading drifted through the hall. "Corpsman, Demerol! Damn-it, Demerol! Demerol!"

Freddie Francis and Lieutenant Honeys

I woke at six the next morning. Someone told me the day's routine called for chow at six-thirty, then an hour's work assignment for the walking wounded, and finally doctors' rounds or muster at nine a.m. Most ambulatory patients had physical therapy assignments sometime during the day. After four-thirty there was overnight liberty for those not restricted by treatment to bed.

Most men of that period went clean-shaven unless at sea or in combat conditions that prevented such luxuries. Freddie Francis was an exception. He made his entrance at about the time I returned from the head and finished making my bunk. He was navy, twenty-seven, and one of about six sailors in Ward 111's count of sixty patients. His left jumper sleeve displayed two red four-year hash marks and a 2nd class aviation mechanic shield. A well-shaped handlebar mustache added a rakish appeal to his Fred Astaire entrance.

Freddie was blond, thin as a weed, and his pale skin tinted toward mustard. Those who knew him said Freddie had managed to do a thirty-year job of pickling his liver in only nine years. He wore a walking cast from below the right knee down. Freddie twirled his cane, nodded, winked, and greeted each patient he passed. At the nurses' station he saluted the lieutenant with a hand kiss and spoke loud enough for the entire ward to hear. "Good morning, Lieutenant Honeys. Yuh looking lovely. Sleep well?"

The nurse glanced up from paperwork. "Good morning, Freddie. Thanks. You sleep at all?" She smiled.

Francis stabbed the air with his cane, pointing at a bedridden marine with an IV in his arm. He saluted, touching the front of his cap with his cane. "Let me be the first to wish you, my war-weary friend, a Mele Kalikimaka eia he´I Hau´oli Makahiki Hou." He waved an arm. "For any of you jar-heads that have led a protected life, that's Hawaiian for 'Merry Christmas and a Happy New Year.'"

The mustached sailor saluted left-handed at a sergeant sitting nearby.

The sergeant sat attired in dress uniform. His cane leaned against the neat bunk. Near the cane was a large manila envelope.

"Hey, Sergeant'te, looking good. What's up?"

"Finally got orders to report to the review board. Look a little peaked, Freddie, what's her name?"

Freddie wagged a finger at the sergeant. "Never to worry, Sergeant'te. Never to worry, my boy. When you get over in them Carolinas, tell 'em hey for old Freddie. You know upper Carolina's home."

"Upper?"

"Sho, the word north will get your mouth washed over there." Freddie dragged the o and dropped the r in north. "You see an old man sitting on a porch drinking a mint julep out of a quart can, it's Grandpa." His drawl treated quart similar to north.

The flight mechanic hooked his cane on the foot of the bunk next to me and took a seat on the chair on its other side. He glanced my way. "Just get in?"

I leaned over the bed between us and we shook. "Yeah, I'm Murdock, Mackey Murdock."

"Freddie Francis. Welcome to the Elephant Grounds."

"Elephant Grounds?"

"Yeah, Elephant Grounds. You read much?"

"Some."

"Man, that's all that makes it worthwhile, books, broads, and booze. I got eleven more years to do then, Mexico, here I come. You know you kin live good on retirement pay down there."

"Can you?"

"Yeah, well that's for me. I'm gonna lie in the shade and sip margaritas while one of them little soft-eyed señoritas reads to me. Anyway I read once, elephants go to a secret place when they're sick or dying. That's what we got here. This is where our guys go. This bunch licks wounds and swaps lies, tries to top the last story told."

"I've heard some of that elephant legend. What happened to that leg?" I worked at getting dressed in my "civvies."

"Sort of mixed a motorcycle with one of them other hobbies I mentioned."

Freddie obviously warmed to his subject and wouldn't be sidetracked. He surveyed the ward while pointing at different guys, telling of their injuries. "Meanwhile, back home, the family's grieving, wondering what happened to their little boys.

They might as well forget it. They'll never get a word. For some reason, folks outside can't understand."

"Meanwhile back here at the grounds, you can't spit it out fast enough. If the wire services had a brain, they'd have somebody out here with a pencil. These guys tell men they just met the whole deal, you know, innermost stuff. Hell, those stories take the better part of the day, every day, and nobody tells one twice."

Nearby a man in a body cast had rowed himself up the aisle on a gurney. He lay on his belly and used two walking canes for oars. The only free part of his body was his arms. The cast started below his knees and stopped at his neck. His face, head, feet, and armpits were visible. A towel covered his butt. I didn't want to consider the consequences indicated by that arrangement. He stopped a couple of beds away to listen.

Freddie smoothed the waxed ends of his mustache. He nodded at the new arrival. "Most keep the stories straight, though some do embellish a little. Still, you never know, there may be a guy in the next bed who knows more about what happened in a certain place than the one telling the story.... Quiet men of war, hell. We're worse than a bunch of old women at a baby shower."

The man in the body cast raised his head the couple of inches his prison allowed. He rolled his eyes high enough to see my face and smiled.

I nodded, "Howdy."

Freddy continued, playing his role for all in hearing distance. "It's been said, there are moments men live that must be told—moments that create then bury emotions deep as souls. Their telling requires details accurate to the last fly on the first corpse." Freddie waved his arms like a stage actor. "Deeds of heroics and acts born of fear must be related in a matter-of-fact manner, without condemnation or glory. Shit, these stories are probably the best medicine Ward 111 offers. Hell, if the shrinks ever find a name for bullshit and learn how to bottle it, they won't need so much Demerol."

The tall marine from last night's wheelchair race walked, swinging his stiff leg, to the end of my bunk and smiled. He laughed at Freddie.

"Francis, you missed your calling. Instead of a grease monkey, you should have been a preacher, or at least a shrink."

"Uh-huh, maybe I'll find a señorita with a typewriter." Francis leaned back and blew smoke rings.

The man on the gurney tilted his head slightly at Francis. "Don't pay no attention to Francis. They made the mistake of circumcising him when they should have clipped his tongue."

The tall marine waited for the chuckling to subside. "Don't think we met last night even though ole Pruitt and I nearly ran you down." He stuck his hand my way. "I'm Bobby Don Hall. What's with the civvies?"

I told my crazy story. They nodded, listened, then invited me to chow. For the first time since boarding the plane, some of the ice in the pit of my stomach melted. Being around these guys sort of washed away all the bullshit. Yeah, they were okay, top-drawer. It felt good to be comfortable again. I had the feeling they knew and were trying to put the rookie, me, at ease.

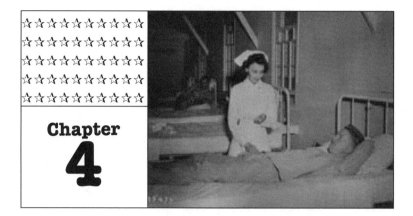

Where's Your Horse, Cowboy?

In the ward, if you laid on your bunk, your head rested inches from the wall; actually, depending on the centering of the bed, it might be a window. On your left side if you looked up the ward the nurses' station caught your eye. If you were on your right, down at the end of the ward, you noticed closed-in rooms. I believe there were two on either side of the aisle. I never heard them given a name, but everyone knew these were for the more seriously ill patients. In my six months stay only one patient was assigned there. After thirty-six hours they carried him out with a blanket over his face. I never learned his name.

Beyond the dying room, a screen-enclosed porch was attached to the south end of Ward 111. Hall, Pruitt, the guy rowing his way through life on the gurney, and I smoked there after the doctors' rounds on my first day at Corpus. The Navy's Blue Angels drill team screamed past, almost kissing each other with their wingtips. It was my first time to see them, other than in newsreels, and I did my best to act indifferent. They made their runs to the south and west of the base. Francis had moved out to supervise a work detail after muster, and a marine staff sergeant named Richards sat nearby.

My attention drifted from the planes to the man on the gurney. At chow I'd asked the others about his injury. "You mean the goldbrick. Oh, he says his back hurts. He's trying for a medical."

How could they be sure, I wondered? I shook my head and took a long draw on the Chesterfield. Poor bastard.

Pruitt walked without a limp, yet, when sitting, preferred a wheelchair. In his hands they became a hot rod, a toy. A wheelchair was to Pruitt what a cane was to Freddie, an extension of his personality. He balanced them on one wheel, made them rear like a mounted circus act, won races with them, and in general, preferred sitting in one to all other forms of comfort. He sat in one in the cool of that porch.

Bobby Don Hall called Marshall, Texas, home. He turned from watching the planes. "Did I ever tell you guys about the first time I ran into the 7th Cav.?

We all shook our heads.

"Well, we were green, I mean raw. We'd landed at Masan, Korea. My combat boots still had a fresh smell to them, and the nearest I'd been to a firefight was listening to what sounded like, but I knew not to be, thunder. Now that storm sounded closer every few yards we covered.

"Well, we were marching north then the word came to fall out beside the road and let a motorized column pass, going south. I'd gotten sprawled out comfortable and lit up when this deuce-and-a-half stops right in front of me. It was headed away from that thunder and the direction we'd all like to be going. The canvas on this thing is rolled back, and it's full of cavalry, I mean standing room only. I look at the truck then at their patches and see 7th Cavalry insignias all over the place.

"You talk about somebody ready for a little R & R; these guys looked used up. They were dirty, unshaven, and unsmiling. They looked like they'd not slept in a month, you know eyes sunk back in their faces and sweat, dust, and mud all over."

Hall paused, looked around for a butt-can, and threw a strike into the one sitting by the screen door. "The ugliest guy in this outfit leaned on the front end gate. His beard, so black it appeared almost blue, held a layer of dust, and his big square jowls bulged with a wad of tobacco. That 7th Cav. emblem brought memories of Custer and all them Indians. This guy's looking right at me, staring sort of insolent-like.

"'Where's your damn horse, cowboy?' I ask. For just an instant that stare gets even colder.

"'We ate the son of a bitch waiting on you damn jar heads to get here,' he said.

"Then he pursed them ole ugly lips, made a face, and shot the prettiest stream of tobacco the ten feet to my boots you ever saw."

Sergeant Richards chuckled. Pruitt asked, "You let him get away with that?" Hall stood six foot three and, I learned later from horsing around with him, was one of the strongest men I've known.

"The damn truck pulled out just then or I'd a jerked his ass out of there."

Cpl. Hall bunked across the aisle and down a couple of beds from me. Memory says he and Staff Sergeant Richards had bunks near each other. They'd both received serious wounds in Korea. Hall's left him with a stiff knee. Richards lost some mobility of his right arm from a shoulder and chest wound.

Bobby Don and I became close, the kind of special relationship you store away and treasure whether you see each other during the next fifty years or not. He was one of those guys you know is making the world better if he's still around.

His wound had nearly totally healed when I arrived at the hospital. Shortly after we met we drove to Austin one Saturday to see a Texas and Rice football game. Hall wore a leg brace with one end fastened by a strap high on his right thigh. The other end was attached to his shoe. He swung the leg stiffly when he walked. The knee joint had no flexible motion. At this point of his recovery he used a cane.

When we arrived in Austin that day, we walked toward the ticket booth near the stadium. Hall wore his uniform. I was in civvies awaiting a replacement for the clothing I'd lost in the fire. We limped to a halt in back of the ticket line, he with his cane and me on crutches.

The ticket man motioned us forward. Those who noticed us bucking the line didn't seem to mind. I remember the two of us fishing for money and being told by the gentleman manning the booth that our money was no good there; the game was on the house. I don't remember who won, but we enjoyed it. For a while we forgot the war and were helped to do so by others not in uniform remembering it.

After the game we stopped at some dive and had a few beers while watching people dance. We'd hoped to find where the college kids gathered, but since I was only nineteen at the time, we had to restrict our drinking business to an area of town where the bartenders were more interested in money than age.

When we pulled out of Austin it was late. We were both pretty blue. Something about the day had seemed out of place. For some reason, grown men playing football seemed sort of childish. Only a few months away from the college life, still it was as though I lived in a different world. I didn't know where I'd be during those kids' next semester, but I expected problems bigger than a course load.

We watched the headlights eat into the darkness and settled into our own thoughts. A few miles out of town Bobby Don gave me an inkling of what was on his mind.

"Murdock, what do you think? You suppose a guy with a stiff leg can find a girl that will be willing to spend her life with him?"

This fun guy was serious. I wish I could be sure of my retort. I knew Bobby Don was hurting and the pain wasn't physical. He's not around to ask so my memory is all that's available. I probably replied with something like, "Hall, ugly as you are, you're gonna have a lot of trouble finding a lady, but that leg won't be the problem when you do. That ugly face and your bullshit is what'll turn her off."

Around two in the morning we were still on the road. I drove a new Chevy with an automatic transmission. My leg and cast took up the passenger seat. Hall sat sideways in the rear with his stiff leg taking up that seat. The beer, our mood, and the full day worked on us. I could hardly stay awake. Hall's breathing said he slept.

I pulled onto a country road. Hall woke. I saw him in the mirror. He straightened, looking in all directions. "Head call?"

"Yeah and I'm gonna catch an hour's sleep." I drove perpendicular to the highway for about a mile. The road was gravel and I found a crossroad before stopping. In the event local toughs checked us out, I wanted an escape route in either direction.

We remained parked there for a couple of hours. I remained awake for a long time sitting sideways facing the highway a mile up the road. An occasional car pulled from the pavement to that gravel, a mile away. A faint glow from headlights would waft across the Chevy's headliner followed by a slight variation in sound from the road traffic.

Each time that highway noise changed, Bobby Don sat bolt upright, testing the night with every sense available. He would go back to sleep quickly each time, reassured, I suspect, that he was safe in Texas. I'd heard of survival skills, one's senses being brought to peak readiness by battle conditions, but Hall was the first I'd met. If I needed someone to watch my backside, I could think of none better.

We shared the same hospital ward for several months after that night. We spent a lot of time together, probably not the best friends either ever had, still, we were special friends, tied with war's unique binding. I don't remember telling him goodbye when I left the ward for my next assignment, but I'm sure I did. He'd raised a personal question that I carried a long time. I shared memories of him with his widow and son fifty years later.

A War Too Many

While many of America's fighting men arrived in Korea like Cpl. Hall, yet to be baptized by fire, many veterans, sorely tested in World War II, were hurriedly formed into reinforcement units. They were thrust into the difficult and bloody battles that so marked the early days of the Korean War. In most cases these veterans were career military men, reserves, or national guardsmen called to active duty from civilian life. They had military experience desperately needed by our armed forces.

As civilians, many had participated in part-time military units for social reasons or the money; few seriously thought the world to be mad enough to again require their services. Fewer still could have conceived of what they found themselves engaged in during the first twelve months of the war.

Marine Staff Sergeant Hardie Lee Richards of Vera, Texas, was one of those veterans who answered the call to active duty. Like many, he'd served in but escaped without injury the

Second World War five years earlier. I never heard him express bitterness, as did some of his peers, but he did mention being greeted on his hometown street, after returning injured from Korea with, "Howdy, Hardie Lee, you been out of town?"

First Lieutenant Clarence "Bud" Archer was another of those World War II veterans called up during the "Korean Emergency." He had flown B-24s in England during his previous service, and Korea created a need for transport pilots, the truck drivers of the air force. Archer referred to single engine and later jet fighter pilots as the Hollywood types.

He filled a much-needed military role during the Korean War. In our interview during the year 2001, he shifted back from experiences of the 1950s and told of celebrating Hitler's birthday on April 21, 1944, by winning a half-crown bet to a friend while riding out a plane crash in England.

Archer and crew had a B-24 checked out that afternoon to get in some night flying hours. He agreed to allow an instructor to check out a student pilot using his plane and crew. Clarence

Clarence Archer in the cockpit.
Photo courtesy of Clarence Archer

stationed himself in the cockpit crouched behind the student. His flight engineer sat behind the instructor. When the student brought it in for a landing, Archer turned to his engineer and whispered, "I'll bet you a half-crown this guy comes up short of the runway."

He won his bet when the student bounced the plane 100 feet short of the runway. Jarred back into the air, the plane stalled, fell back to earth, and the right gear plowed up mud and runway for yards until the gear finally broke. The instructor pilot had enough presence of mind to kill the power as they dug into the runway, and the plane did not burn in the ensuing crash. It did snag a wing tip, veer out into the rough, and rip itself apart before coming to a stop. Fearing fire or explosion, Archer said he snagged his watch and lost it scrambling out the top hatch. Was the bet paid off? He doesn't remember.

Larry Zellers also served in the air force in the Second World War. Different circumstances found him in Korea in 1950. He was a civilian working in Kaesong, Korea, on June 25, 1950. He heard some of the first shots. The sound only traveled a couple of miles.

Twenty-eight years old and newly married, both Larry and his wife taught school in a Christian supported missionary environment. Larry gave the sounds of gunfire along the 38th parallel little thought that morning. "Just another little border skirmish between North and South Korea," he assumed. It was 4 A.M., and he turned over and tried to go back to sleep.

Later in the morning Zellers and missionary companions watched from his living room window as figures darted about in the early morning fog. At first they mistook them for South Koreans. By afternoon downed utility poles and other damage in the community convinced them of the situation's seriousness. Fortunately, Mrs. Zellers was away. She'd taken ill at a wedding in Seoul the previous weekend. Larry returned home without her, expecting her to follow shortly.

Chapter 5

Four days later Larry Zellers, teacher, missionary worker, and former World War II air force crewman along with a group of five other civilian doctors, nurses, and missionary workers, opened the door to a nice-looking young Korean civilian.

In Larry's words, "The young man was the picture of proper manners. On being asked to sit down, he graciously accepted. Tea and cookies were served.

"He chatted pleasantly then broached his main subject. 'Have you been to the city hall to pay your respects to the new officials?' he inquired."

Thus beguiled, Zellers and his five companions were lured into imprisonment by one young North Korean official. Larry described it. "It was a brilliant performance! One young man unarmed and alone had succeeded in rounding up six Americans and their two vehicles, plus one Korean driver, without firing a shot, without any unpleasantness, and without their even knowing what he was doing. Not only that, but he and the other Communist officials now had the run of two well-stocked American houses to loot at their own convenience."

A few days prior to Larry's arrest, a North Korean soldier had threatened him with death on the street. With bystanders cleared from behind him to avoid the executioner's bullet and the barrel of the soldier's rifle buried in his stomach, Larry discovered death has an odor and a taste.

He said, "Suddenly, I detected a pungent odor like that of scorching hair, and I noticed a strong chemical taste in my mouth. I was to experience them again."

The soldier pulled the trigger and laughed when the rifle snapped on an empty chamber. The cat and mouse game, the cruelty, would become all too familiar. For most victims the rifle's firing pin found a cartridge.

Though Mr. Zellers' actual capture was conducted without unpleasantness, the word falls short in describing the nearly three years of imprisonment. Abuse and interrogation started immediately.

Unlike Larry, PFC Mickey Scott failed to hear the first shots. At the time they sounded, he worked on his second hitch at the Marine Corps Supply Depot, Barstow, California. It took thirty-nine days for Mickey to learn the seriousness of America's fighting men's position in Korea then he grabbed the first opportunity and volunteered to go over as part of a group of reinforcements for the 1st Marines. He arrived at Inchon, Korea, in late September 1950.

After assignment to Dog Co., 2nd Battalion, 7th Marine Regiment of the First Marine Division at Seoul, Mickey's regiment loaded on LSTs at Inchon and sailed around South Korea to Wonsan harbor on the coast of North Korea. ROK forces had arrived before them, yet the harbor was still heavily mined. The last of the enemy resistance would be cleared once the navy swept the harbor clean. The seasick marines spent two weeks sailing the Yellow Sea while the navy handled that chore. Their landing met no resistance.

Mickey and his buddies were anxious to engage the enemy. They'd take care of this thing quickly then head home. Tough as they were, growing accustomed to a country where human excrement was collected for fertilizer and placed from buckets onto fields of rice and gardens of vegetables took some adjustment. Troops who arrived in the summer spoke of greeting the odor well out on the Sea of Japan. Such a source of irritation had to have a name. "Honey buckets" seemed to fit.

Dog Company's first combat came near Sudong-ni on the road to the reservoir. Mickey remembers, "We hit the deck in lots of rice paddies and learned to identify enemy fire by its odd sound. The Communist tracers were green, ours, the U.N., red.

"Soon we were constantly probing. In the corps you learn quickly that defense and forts are for others. The marine's mission is to patrol—patrol and find—seek out and engage the enemy and win the contest before he finds you.

"We found them often. Near the middle of October we rode trucks up the icy plateau to Hagaru. It's located at the reservoir. Soon at Hagaru-ri we found a deserted town except for a very ancient man too worn to travel. Uncomfortable in the eerie silence of this place, we took the old man captive and learned the residents had vanished into the mountains, fleeing the battles."

Mickey and I were sitting in front of a Dairy Queen in Cleburne, Texas. We had not seen each other in thirty years. We'd worked together after the Korean War in the 1960s at Texas Instruments, Inc. in Dallas, Texas. We'd been young, aggressive supervisors there. Age had worked on us some, but the more we talked the more I recognized features almost forgotten of my old friend. When I thought of a book containing oral histories of experiences dealing with the Korean War, Mickey's name had come to mind.

He continued, "Hagaru-ri's population returned the next day. They began working, selling goods and helping us, the conquerors, in any way to survive the bitter winter."

Late in November the war was about to change. U.N. troops began to make contact with advance scouts of Chinese.

Mickey said, "These fighters were dressed in uniforms of loose-fitting clothing which included white, cotton-padded outfits with parkas. They blended well with the snow. Less stealthy than their North Korean allies, still, most of these new enemies faded into the hills when spotted or were eliminated by our fire."

Most troops in Korea were served a hot meal for Thanksgiving on or around the 24th or 25th of November 1950. I asked Mickey about it. The meal was supposed to see the troops through until they could get back to the States for Christmas. "We missed it. We were freezing on a hillside and guarding artillery."

Mickey looked at my messy scribbling as he talked. It seemed the spirits of dead men were around us. I knew he wanted this done absolutely right, perfectly, if at all.

So did I. The lives and events we talked about demanded no less. I regretted my lack of organization, my penmanship. "We'll rewrite it over and over, Mickey. Nothing will be released without both our approvals," I promised.

Mickey continued, "A little later, the company advanced northwest of the reservoir to Yudam-ni and set up a combat base. Third Platoon of Dog Company moved as flank guard, far in advance of the regiment along a ridgeline near the Chosin Reservoir. We had patrolled all day in snow up to our waists, pretty miserable."

"I was in charge of a fire team of four. We skirmished up a ridge with orders to seize and occupy the hill. Near the top the four of us kicked frozen, rock-hard dirt and cussed our miserable lot and inability to see the enemy or dig in. The next instant we moved to the crest and faced more Communist Chinese soldiers than you could shake a stick at. They, too, were moving over the top. Oh, good grief! Geeze, what are we going to do?" Mickey took a deep breath. His voice was hushed. It had been over fifty-one years, and the unbelievable hopelessness of the situation had not diminished.

"Completing the mission was impossible, but perhaps, just maybe, I could save my troops from destruction." Mickey told me earlier that as the PFC in charge he'd surrendered his fire team to the Chinese. You could sense it was a load he'd carried fifty years without apology or regret, just sadness at its necessity.

"Chinese appeared to our front over the rim of the hill. They held burp guns and grenades at the ready and walked within ten or twenty feet, jabbering and motioning for us to run." Now he was telling the details. He repeated his words from long ago, and I wondered how many times they'd burned through his memory. "'Alright guys, lay 'em down easy.' Each man bent and gently laid down his rifle. This trip we had no BAR man. We'd probably have died on the spot if we'd had one.

"They opened fire on us, point blank, but one guy and I dove backward off the ridge. At that point the world exploded about us. Corsairs screamed overhead, firing directly into the hill and the Chinese. They blew that ridge into dust. Parts of bodies were flying all over. Our would-be captors went nuts, running, firing in all directions, at the planes, the company, and us.

"The F-4 Us made pass after pass, firing everything they had. I learned later, thank God, they'd run out of napalm earlier so cannons, machine guns, and rockets were their only choice. The company had marked us off and targeted close air support on top of our position now occupied by the Chinese. Tactically it was proper; personally it was a bad place to be.

"We were in snow up to our belts, cold, near frozen, being shot at by our guys from the air, the company, and an advancing army of Chinese, some from only thirty feet away. A Chinese machine gun rattled just a short distance from us, spraying the area.

"The private with me was bleeding from wounds all over." Mickey stopped and took a deep breath. "I bent over this guy, but I had nothing to help him. I told him, 'You gotta get back to the company for aid. I think they are that way. Tell 'em... say, if they charge these guys, I've still got two hand grenades and a bayonet. I'll try to get that machine gun.'

"Then, I'm alone, lying in snow up to my chin, thinking to myself I must do something to rid myself of being a target. I'm about to freeze to death, but, strange as it sounds, I was calm and relaxed.

"The Corsairs kept up their strafing and boy were they good. When they passed overhead, the Chinese would turn their fire back in my direction. Finally the planes left and things got quiet for several hours. A Chinese wearing white appeared with a Tommy gun, and I slowly stood up and raised my hands. I scared the pants off him. I never saw a guy so startled in my life. He thought there was nothing around but the dead. That mountain, that ridgeline was nothing but blood. For years I felt, with a strange calmness, that I actually died that day near a little hamlet named Kyodong-ni.

"They walked me off that bloody hill to a farmhouse. It had a potato storage hole about ten feet in diameter and ten feet deep with a roof on it. They put me in there with other prisoners captured throughout the night. It was the 27th of November 1950, the night the communists attacked the 1st Marines Division that was dug in at Yudam-ni, Hagaru-ri, and Koto-ri. The fight continued to Hamhung on the Yellow Sea."

Now a prisoner, Mickey missed that action. His captors marched him a different direction.

Cpl. Bobby Don Hall wrote his mother his impression of the marines of the 7th Regiment that were a part of that 1st Marine Division Mickey spoke of. He joined them shortly after their evacuation from Hungnam. He had landed a few days earlier on December 18, 1950, at Masan.

Hall's widow read me the letter. His son sat nearby. He wrote, "You talk about a bunch of ragged, beat-up guys. Yesterday I saw the 7th Marine Regiment. They were a part of the 1st Marine Division that had to fight its way out from the Chosin Reservoir a few days ago. Out of 2,100 men only this handful made it back. Mom, they were beat-up, but not beat. They were still proud, hurt but proud."

Mickey Scott continued. "By morning there were eleven of us in that hole. There were two navy corpsmen, a wounded sergeant, a reserve corporal, and counting myself, seven more marines. We stayed there a few days then we started walking under guard. Of the eleven, four of us eventually came home. I repeat the names of all eleven of those guys a couple of times each month."

"Where is Everybody?"

Three days after getting married, Ed Miller received orders to active duty in the marine reserves. It was July 28, 1950. On September 15 he landed with the 1st Marine Division, 11th Regiment, at Inchon. He was part of the 4th Battery, 155mm Howitzer Battalion.

In the summer of 2001 we shared the privacy of his upstairs office in his home. The view overlooked a beautiful golf course near Frisco, Texas. He spoke: "We rode through Seoul on trucks pulling these 155mms. At one time I was the Old Man's radioman. He was good, really cool under fire.

"Word came down of an enemy position. He gets his driver and me and says, 'Come on, boys, let's go take a look.' We pile in a jeep and get within sight of this Korean pillbox. It is in the side of a mountain. We are in fairly open country and it's there in front of us. The captain squints at that thing while calculating in his mind then called back, 'What are you firing?'

"He gets his answer, calls back the coordinates, and replies, 'Fire for effect.' The first one lands and he says change to this, this, and this. Then zap there's no pillbox.

"It gets quiet. 'Good, let's get back to the line, Captain,' one of us says. That man had no fear." Ed Miller exudes self-assurance. Our time together had been short, but I felt at ease and comfortable that any experiences shared by this man would be unpretentious.

"We loaded back aboard ship again and sailed around to Korea's other coast. At Hungnam they were clearing mines like crazy so we bypassed it and landed up the coast. Trucks started us on a slow haul north toward Yudam-ni.

"The roads in the mountains turned to ice, but when we arrive at Toktong Pass it's passable and the Turks have it open. We got up to Yudam-ni then on November 27 the word came down that we were surrounded. It was cold, 30 degrees below zero or something like that. The breech on our heavy guns opened slowly if at all. It was just too cold for them to function properly. We made it back to Koto-ri on December 4, 1950, and it was about there that I took a round on the helmet that barely grazed me but almost broke my neck. I had the chinstrap fastened."

Sergeant Louis Holmes of the 7th Infantry Division also fought the cold near the Chosin Reservoir. "We were sent out on a night patrol to find the enemy. We found them. They wore white, white pants, jackets, and parkas. We couldn't tell if they were North Koreans or Chinese, but there were a lot of them. The night grew bitter cold!

"I knew enough not to take a direct route back to our lines because we didn't want them to follow us home. We suffered badly from the white-hot cold of frostbite later, but we finally made it in. I'm more fatigued than I realize, had probably sweated heavy in my inner clothing. Down in this hole I shake and suffer then after a while everything turns more and more peaceful.

"Next, I'm in this dark warm tunnel, perfectly at peace just staring into this beautiful light. Then rough hands are pulling at me, massaging my body and interrupting my peace. I fuss, but they keep it up, working to maintain blood circulation. Any rate, I got married a few months later in house shoes nursing frost-bitten feet."

Reverend and Mrs. Holmes celebrate thirty years of pastoring Bethel Baptist Church in September 1992. They started with a pen pal relationship.

I missed the time line on the details of his story, but at some point Ed Miller volunteered to go back to a hill near Yudam-ni to retrieve dead and wounded. He would serve as armed guard, sort of riding shotgun for a helicopter rescue mission. The rest of his outfit joined an infantry group making its way south.

"The choppers of that day wouldn't carry much weight. We'd load casualties on board and they'd leave us on that hill while they flew them out. While the choppers were gone we went over to help some guys with a truckload of frozen corpses." Miller paused, shuffled something on his desk. "They were sort of like cordwood, stiff. We'd toss them on as respectfully as possible.

"With the guys working at the truck, we numbered about twenty. Somebody looked around and asked, 'Where is everybody?' We all looked around. We must have been the last twenty guys out of Yudam-ni. We finally got down to the road with others who were using it for protection.

"I remember coming to a place where the terrain leveled out, and across this flat area almost nothing was getting through. We got partway across and were sort of pinned down. We looked back and here came a truck loaded with wounded across that flat. A Chinese machine gunner killed the driver and started killing the wounded. The truck just sort of made a jerking halt, still running.

"The guy next to me says, 'If you'll cover me, I'm going to get that truck.' He takes off and I'm firing.

"A mortar round came in close, bent me over, and sprayed me with shrapnel. I fell off the hill and lost vision but didn't think I was bad hurt, just scratches and bruised some."

Ed continued. "I lean forward, trying to see and hear somebody say, 'He got the truck!'

"The guy at the truck hollers. 'Come on, can you make it?'

"'I don't know,' I holler.

"'You better damn sure find out,' he says.

"Well somehow I get down to the truck and am holding on, stumbling along while this guy in the cab is peeking over the dash about once every few minutes. Bullets plink into that thing from every direction. It ends up with me running along-side holding on in snow and ice. He hits the ditch, I fall, and the next thing I know those back dual wheels go right over the top of both my legs, smashing my ass into that snow. Now I've had it! It passes on over me, but I can't move.

"I feel hands on me then I'm sailing through the air and I land up on top of that canvas that's stretched over the hoops. They literally threw me on top of the thing then we move on out and into momentary protection from a slight rise.

"We get to Hagaru-ri and some guys haul me up to a C-46 sitting there with props spinning. The door is open and a voice from inside hollers, 'We got room for one more man.' Again I fly through the air, literally thrown aboard."

When war cracks like frozen spittle about starving, exhausted, and frostbitten men, the courage to go on must come from deep within. The living who marched from Chosin through a gauntlet of fire, carrying their dead and wounded, reached a plateau of heroics seldom achieved. The cause being defended by the United Nations paid dearly. Humanity prospered greatly.

A sergeant from the 7th Regiment of the Third Infantry Division moved north on the marines' left flank toward Chosin. His name is George Zonge. An army thirty-year man, he was in charge of a weapons platoon. They fought back to Hungnam. He brought up the rear.

Zonge says in Rudy Tomedi's history of the Korean War, *No Bugles, No Drums*, "At Hungnam the navy was evacuating everybody. It was just one big swamp of slush and mud, from all the vehicles and troops going through. The air was full of smoke from burning factories and warehouses.

"I think they evacuated the troops alphabetically. I helped set the charges on the docks, and the guy helping me was named Zimmer. Zimmer and Zonge! I don't believe that was a coincidence because he was a captain and I was a sergeant.

Goodbye Hungnam!
Photo courtesy of Ed Buckman USN

It was a spectacular explosion. We piled up cases of frozen dynamite and all the extra ammo and gas drums and wired it together and set it off with primacord. The explosion almost capsized the transport I was aboard in the bay when it went off.

The first months of the Korean War coupled with the Chosin Reservoir campaign of 1950 devoured a lot of U.S. men, equipment, and strength. Like Dunkirk in World War II, it required a mighty effort from all available resources, and heroic deeds from fighting men of all branches of the service were the order of the day. Victory, defeat, advance, retreat have little meaning compared to the reality of courage and the nearness of eternity such a time drapes around both the living and the dead. Monuments of frozen corpses from both sides stared through sightless eyes as the last swirls of smoke curled from the refuse of war. Forces of the U.N. moved out to sea from Hungnam, determined to regroup, replenish, and return.

Chapter 7

The Dean's Conflict

In the winter of 1950, about the time Mickey started walking as a prisoner, the Dean of Men at North Texas State College in Denton, Texas, Dr. "Dean" Woods, fought mixed emotions. His role had always been to assist and encourage young men to stay in college and maintain low turnover among the male students. Now, three students presented him with a dilemma. The three were Bill Mackey, one-time president of the college's student government, Carl Kisinger, a junior from Seymour, and I, a sophomore.

Bill, the oldest of the three and on a first-name basis with the dean as a result of his role in student government, carried the conversation. He told Dr. Woods of the pact we'd agreed to that called for each to drop out of school at the end of the semester and volunteer for the military. The Korean War news worsened daily. Our friends not in college or deferred for other reasons were being drafted and sent to battle as fast as the government could process them.

Bill finished, "We'd like to have your thought about this, Dean."

Dean Woods fiddled with a letter opener and looked out the window. I could almost read the thoughts going through the man's mind. The dean nodded and took a deep breath. A conflict existed between the needs of his country and the college that

Bill Mackey packed light between wars.

employed him. He talked around the subject, avoiding a direct answer. After all the man would have to live with 20-20 hindsight if any of us failed to return. He finally came back to the critical question. "In spite of your college deferment, you guys feel a duty, a responsibility, to enlist?"

"Something like that," Bill replied. "Probably, nearer the truth would be that we are bored with school and ready to see a little scenery."

Dean Woods laughed. His eyes twinkled. The old fox had seen through our BS. He'd found the truth. The three of us knew Korea might still be there when we graduated. Who wanted to take a chance on slogging through rice paddies and sleeping in a cold hole in the ground? Responsibility, hell! This was survival. Naw, we'd just get a good, warm, safe berth on a ship somewhere while seeing a few ports and waiting out the war. Someone else could drag his ass through Korea. It'd be the navy for us.

The dean stood. "You boys have a question too heavy for me to address. I'll tell you this, though, if you do go, I'd give nearly anything to be young enough to go with you."

My family had a good Christmas in 1950 then I brought the sadness of the war to my parents a few nights later. I told them I planned to drop out of college between semesters and join the navy. The break between fall and spring semesters was only a couple of weeks off. My high school pals were being drafted at a rapid rate. Other than that I could think of little to say. Mom cried all that night. I'm not sure about the next. Dad said, "Whatever you do, don't volunteer for anything."

None of us knew Larry Zellers then. He spent that Christmas as a prisoner of the atheistic North Korean Communists. By that time he'd seen many deaths and suffered terribly himself. They were at Hanjang-ni and were allowed to join with other prisoners consisting of Muslims, Russian Orthodox Christians, Catholics, a Jew, and Protestants in singing

Christmas carols. He described the night in his book *In Enemy Hands*. "There was peace at Hanjang-ni that Christmas Eve; for a few golden moments we shut out the wickedness of that place. The light shone on those of us who sat in darkness and in the shadow of death."

There was no peace for Mickey Scott that Christmas. He starved, stumbled, slipped, and struggled to stay alive on icy mountain trails. The average age of his fellow prisoners grew younger with time as the older ones died on a death trail to a Chinese prison.

Back at college, the final week of the semester was busy. Carl and Bill finished a day before me. Carl and I woke up the morning of my last test and found Bill's note. It said something about, "Gone to the navy, see you when the war's over"—something like that.

I left the dorm to take my test. Carl and I had talked about wishing we could only go in for the duration instead of a four-year hitch. Otherwise, there was always the possibility we'd find ourselves spending a year or so in the peacetime navy after the war was over.

The exam was in two parts. A classmate and I went outside to smoke at the break. I lit a cigarette for this guy, and the talk turned to Korea. He mentioned the naval reserve in Dallas and that he had joined.

He said, "You can join the reserve for four years, then request active duty, effective as soon as you complete two weeks of boot camp this summer. You only have to sign for active duty for the duration of the war."

It was what we'd been looking for, a chance for the navy and still get out as soon as the war was over. I finished the test and ran the mile back to the dorm. I took the stairs two at a time to Carl's upstairs room. His letter lay on his bed—same story—"See you when the war's over." I was too late.

There I was, in my mind, the last civilian. I joined the reserve the next day, put my name in for active duty as soon as possible, and went back to college. I was not a good student that semester. I wasn't much of a civilian either, certainly not a good citizen. I couldn't even have a good time. Everything was on hold. I didn't know Mickey Scott or Larry Zellers then. I knew somewhere guys like me were dying, but I couldn't relate to it. Today, I think, I like myself a little better for the guilt I suffered that next semester, waiting to hold up my end of that stupid pact.

I make no evaluation of what others did or didn't do during that time or in other conflicts. This is just the way I found it in 1950s thinking. Some may label our generation, not as the one that fought the Korean War, but as the one victimized by the propaganda of World War II. We were "ate up" with the John Wayne image.

Hollywood had done a number on us that soon wore off. We found war different from the way we'd played it in the early forties as children. Some complained no one knew the Korean War was going on. It's even been called the "forgotten war." In all honesty, I was more concerned that as an individual I might be forgotten than I was of any nonchalance concerning the war itself—that and the fact we could be drafted but couldn't buy a beer or vote.

Perhaps the lack of a nationally mobilized effort at psychological persuasion was not all bad. Maybe the next generation's vision was less clouded. Maybe they taught us something.

Whatever conclusion history puts on that issue, it will not diminish one iota the honor, the courage, and the nobility of those who gave their blood during all our country's struggles of the past century.

Pruitt's Chariot

Pruitt said goodbye to his wheelchair and accepted a ride home. It was near Christmas, 1951. He, Staff Sergeant Hardie Lee Richards, and another guy whose name escapes me joined in the trip from Corpus. After a couple of hours' travel, we were north of San Antonio and in the Hill Country. Shadows lengthened. Our initial energy burst at being on the road and away from the hospital had worn off; we traveled now in silence, each with our own thoughts.

Someone, I believe it was Pruitt himself, had told me how he received his wound. He'd jumped out of a tank to get ammunition during a firefight while providing close support to infantry. The tank crew had run out of ammunition for their automatic weapons. He'd opened the hatch but had not gone far when a blast from a communist burp gun almost cut him in half. Various stories went around the ward as to how many feet of his intestines the doctors removed. Unless I find the Fort Worth native, I'm afraid to say, but his wound was severe.

That evening he looked toward the fading light at the high ridgeline looming to our left. "Just think," he said, "not a damn gook up there."

I let Pruitt out somewhere in Fort Worth. I don't remember going to his house or if I gave him a lift on the return trip to Corpus. His comment, when he returned to the ward, however, burns in my mind.

A buddy asked. "How was home, Pruitt? Did they give you a hero's welcome?"

Pruitt looked at the guy and answered slowly. "Home, Christmas, too, was fine. They were glad to see me, but, no, it had nothing to do with heroes. They only come home in boxes."

I wish I could find him. To think I started out measuring that guy by the pound. I wish I knew his first name.

An appearance before a review board was scheduled before separation from the service for marines whose wounds were serious enough to prevent returning to active duty. The board was located in Charleston, South Carolina. There they decided the monetary value to place on disability—so much for an arm, another amount for a leg.

Guys like Pruitt caused us to speculate if the amount of his check would be relative to the length of intestines he lost. Imagine the poor devils performing such assignments. The government probably gave them a list, dollars on one side, organs on the other.

Kenneth L. Wilkinson, a marine PFC in A Co., 1st Marine Brigade, 5th Regiment, also tangled with a North Korean burp gun. He doesn't remember what happened next but did show a sharp edge when the physical review board was mentioned in conversation. "Yeah, an eye was worth 40 percent of base pay. I knew a guy who lost both eyes. They gave him 80 percent and a dog."

As the years went by and modern medicine did so much in terms of prosthesis development, I found myself wondering from time to time if Hall ever received a replacement for the knee he lost. I learned in 2001 that he died in 1987. His widow said they tried a few things for his knee over the years, but he got no relief. She also mentioned Bobby Don had an ongoing struggle with the government concerning the amount of his disability entitlement.

Sometimes when you go hunting the truth you just find too damn much.

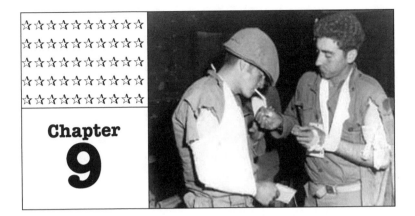

To Steal a Cow

The war was in its last months when Glen Thompson of the 25th Infantry Division, 14th Regiment, Company H arrived in Inchon, Korea. Later he found himself in a blocking position behind Pork Chop Hill. It was the last months, but people were still dying. An argument could be made that in eternity the freshness of the dirt on the grave makes little difference, and it's about all that separates the first from the last killed.

"We'd been on the line in the same uniform for almost forty days. We'd had one bath during that time then we finally got sent back to this holding position. They passed the word almost as soon as we got there. 'There'll be an inspection at 09:00 tomorrow. Clean 'em up and line 'em up.'

"You can imagine how happy we were with that. Well, a section sergeant in our machine gun platoon slips over to the mortar platoon's area and urinates into the mouth of this spit and polished 'piss-tube' (mortar) they had out there for the old man's inspection.

"Later at chow our CO hears us cackling and laughing at this. He gets the picture and doesn't find it funny. He sort of chastises us in that mild way COs have and invites us to accompany him over to the mortar area where he tells them the guilty ones are there to polish and clean weapons for them just as long as they wished."

You wouldn't expect to find a lot of comedy in war, but the energy of youth will not be denied. The following stories I either witnessed or heard others tell for the truth. Some I heard so often I believe them to be more legend than fact. Even if I knew the owners of all these tales, still, on occasion, I'd have to plead the fifth or suffer momentary memory lapses.

A shipmate and I once decided, while awaiting a boat to return to our anchored ship, to commandeer one of the civilian water taxis secured nearby at the dock in Vallejo, California. It was about 2 a.m. Our ship, the LST-1146, was tied up down river about three or four miles. The taxi was used to ferry shipyard workers during shift changes to and from the Mare Island Naval Base. Built like oversize whaleboats, they carried dozens of workers across the river.

The current at this spot is swift and treacherous. The boat was securely tied fore and aft with ropes, but nowhere was there a lock. My buddy enjoyed more knowledge of diesel mechanics than common sense so there'd be no trouble getting the engine started. I began removing the lines while he worked with the engine. We laughed, imagining the expressions on the faces of our buddies when we came roaring up like Admiral of the Fleet in our own launch. We gave no thought to the look that might be worn by the officer of the deck.

I had the stern line off and was on the last wrap of the bowline when my buddy hollered. "Hold it, Murdock, they've taken the damn battery."

I managed to get the stern pulled back around and secured then we waited for our own boat. Luck more than good sense allowed me to grow old. They'd have had to pipe sunlight to us had some thoughtful civilian not taken the battery from his boat that night.

The friend with me had spent six months in the stockade in Japan before I joined the ship's crew. I won't give you his name. I will tell you I was not surprised to recently learn he's now a church minister in Arkansas, still shepherding flocks through treacherous water. Most of his congregation would, I'm sure, be forgiving, but there may be one or two who fail to understand the power of redemption. On second thought, I'm not sure he required any deliverance. His presence at the invasion of Inchon, Korea, proved his readiness to lay down his life for his countrymen. In those immortal words from *Cool Hand Luke*, the stockade deal only showed a "failure to communicate."

In my book *Last of the Old-Time Texans*, the late Bill Mann of Waco, Texas, related a story of a buddy he went ashore with in Normandy who had a nose for eggs. The short version of the story is that the man rolled on the ground with pockets full of a local farmer's eggs while trying to get a shot at a German sniper. When the action was over, the soldier remembered his hen fruit and started feeling of his clothing to determine the damage. To everyone's surprise he had not broken an egg. The comedy and relief of the occasion, only hours away from Omaha beach, gave Bill's outfit a moment of hysterical relief at the time and caused Bill to laugh uncontrollably when he relayed the story to me fifty-six years later.

A marine in the Corpus Naval Hospital told of stealing a Korean cow. His bunch had an urge for fresh steak and spotted a farmer's cow across a river in Korea. He and two other marines decided to do a little rustling. They located a couple of guys who agreed to butcher and cook the cow if these guys would bring her in. They had the cow in tow at mid-river, when all hell broke loose.

57

According to this joker seven nations did their best to interrupt their "tomfoolery." French, Turks, Americans, South Koreans, English, North Koreans, and Chinese all converged on the river and started a hell of a battle. "They fired salvo after salvo across that river, just over our heads. That was the slowest damn cow I ever saw," he said then added, "and the skinniest."

After the war I met an ex-soldier who had slogged over a good part of Korea. He told a story that never failed to bring laughter among veterans and looks of disbelief from civilized folks.

He said, "I was tired of living in a hole without a bath and testing the breeze with a bare-ass each time I relieved myself. We'd been on the line since I couldn't remember when. I figured I'd taken enough.

"Well a fresh engineering outfit moved in a ways behind us. I decided to give them a visit. This outfit lived with luxuries only engineers could come up with. They even had a new wooden one-hole outhouse.

"I couldn't resist. It'd been too long. I had to try that thing. Well when I stepped out, stuffing my shirttail and straightening my belt, this damn corporal starts in on me.

"He says I can just, 'keep the hell away from their privy.' They weren't in Korea, 'to provide latrines for every lost dog-face that strolled down the pike.' Furthermore, he'd like nothing better than to just whip my ass and that's exactly what he'd do next time he caught me on their premises.

"Well he was too big for me to fight, and I couldn't shoot the son of a bitch because others of his outfit were looking on. I just turned around like a whipped pup and headed back for the front, thinking all the time I had to have a plan. Well, by the time I got back to our bunker, I had it worked out.

"I went back down that hill the next morning. Damned if someone didn't toss a grenade through the half-moon vent of that crap house sometime during the night. That engineering marvel was reduced to toothpicks." When asked if it had been occupied the GI was vague.

After the war I downed a few beers with an ex-army sergeant who served in Korea. This guy saw a lot of war and came home to the bumpy road of civility. He was a good draftsman and, while still in Korea and as a veteran of considerable combat, was assigned to work on battlefield maps. The scene I pictured from his description of his workplace was of an almost empty, cold barracks with his wooden table and a chair at one end and a lot of miserable Korean nothingness at the other.

He said, "From time to time officers would come by and check out maps or maybe just get a new officer oriented. Well the place wasn't far from the line. It was dirty, and I matched it well. I carried a bayonet and a forty-five on my belt and kept my M-1 leaning by the door. I didn't shave often, and a bath while there was a rare luxury.

"I had this thing going with a rat that made an appearance at the other end of the barrack each morning. His ritual was to come out of his hole, scamper a little ways, then slow down for a moment then speed up and head for his exit. Well, each day he did this I'd pull my bayonet and throw it at this damn thing. This has been going on for weeks. I ain't hit nothing, yet. After a while I get to where I take the sticker out and lay it beside my maps to be ready for this guy. It's getting personal.

"When it happens, it's like it had been staged. These officers came by. There were two of them that I saw regularly. They had a new lieutenant with them and introduced him to me. The guy still had a States smell to him. He's all eyes when one of the others asks for a certain map.

"I catch a movement out of the corner of my eye at the other end of the room. My bayonet is lying on the table. With a nonchalant motion I pick it up and flip the thing at Mr. Rat. It pins him so neat to the far wall you wouldn't believe it. That bayonet just about made two of him. Out of the corner of my eye, the lieutenant is sizing me up like maybe I'm Jim Bowie.

"Well, I have to finish my act. I stand up, walk to the other end, retrieve my sticker, and wipe that filthy stuff on the leg of my fatigues. I go back and pull the map they wanted to see. These two older officers are on to the whole thing. They are about to pop, but that young guy is straining to see that map from as far away from me as he can stand."

The story was fresh on this guy's mind when I used to hear him tell it and even after a few beers only brought a slight grin to his face. As with most returning veterans, time, training wheels, and a little rehabilitation was needed to bring back expressions of relaxed fun and unclouded joy to his face.

Events Burned in Memory

My ex-sergeant friend wasn't alone in finding it difficult to smile during early adjustment to a peacetime world. Others, including POW Mickey Scott experienced years with little reason to express pleasure.

Mickey and I worked together in the 1960s. In 2001 we sat in my van and shared his experiences as a POW. We were parked beside a Dairy Queen in Cleburne, Texas. He talked. I took notes. We were wrapping up three hard hours for Mickey. I'd not found them easy, myself. He had just relived, in memory, years spent with the Communist Chinese while a POW.

People went in and out of the goody shop near us. Grinning children carried ice cream. Mickey shook his head. "So many young men caught up in that war, just kids really. So many wasting away. It seems unbelievable now to think of two and a half years with nothing to smile about."

A moment later he turned, and we discussed details for later sessions. I had the impression that, as difficult as reliving those days was for Mickey, he felt good about what we were doing. Still, I had reservations. I questioned my ability, my motives, and most of all, the invasion into others' privacy a work of this kind demands.

I'd not bled as had many of the men I interviewed, had not suffered as had most. I'd not known months of no laughter. The old survivor guilt dug at my insides. In Pruitt's words, I'd not "died." There were always others who had contributed more.

I was a week away from meeting Larry Zellers at Weatherford, ten days from reading his book *In Enemy Hands*. In this excellent book he unknowingly addressed my concerns. He wrote of wondering, as a prisoner, when others died around him, if he had energy to survive—had he failed to do all possible for the dying.

"Could I have given more of my own food to the starving and survived?" he asked himself.

He wrote of the winter of 1950 as a prisoner at Hanjang-ri. "The next morning, November 25, Monsignor Quinlan got up early to check on Bishop Byrne. When he returned a few minutes later, he called out through the closed door to Father Booth, 'Will'm, Pat's gone to heaven.'

"Later that morning Monsignor Quinlan and a few of us buried Bishop Byrne in one of the last few graves that we were able to dig in the fast-freezing earth. The Monsignor had earlier placed a light cassock with metal buttons on the body, which he hoped would make it possible to identify the remains at a later time. After conducting a brief funeral service, he turned to me and asked, 'Larry, do you think you will ever be able to remember this place?'

"I stood up and looked around me. 'Monsignor, I don't think I'll ever be able to forget it.'"

Larry continued. "Those contemplating writing a tribute to the life of a great man would be well advised—or so I tell myself—to consider the matter carefully: Are you in possession of the pertinent information regarding his life, and do you have the consummate skill to put it on paper? If not, then you had better leave that task to others. Yet it is unthinkable at this point in my story not to observe the passing of Bishop Patrick Byrne with some small note of tribute, however inadequate."

I have reread Larry's words many times. They knife through my facade of toughness. I wish I'd written them. They bring me some degree of peace. Yes, as long as I have some assurance that those of whom I write or their survivors hunger for others to remember the personal experiences and thoughts related here, it is unthinkable not to bring it forth. Fragmented by time and dulled by aging memories, still it is fitting, as Larry mentioned, to pay tribute, "however inadequate," to their legacy.

Mickey's comments that day at the Dairy Queen reinforce Larry's written words. We shook hands as we were about to separate. "I guess that's it for the day, unless I take you home with me," he said. I'm going to take that to mean he agrees the time is ripe for these tales to be aired.

Mickey told of leaving his potato-hole prison in December 1950. "You talk about a death march, we walked about four months, I don't know exactly how long. We'd walk at least thirty miles each night, mostly over slippery mountain trails. Then in the daytime we'd hole up to avoid attack from U.N. planes. Before long the number of older POWs began to dwindle. They'd died from one or a combination of age, wounds, lack of spirit, food, and climate.

"These Chinese weren't so brutal, just strict and rigid. It was just that they had nothing, no food, no medicine, and no place to house prisoners. One would come up and take our few items, look at them, then give them back. Later they quit giving items back. Every once in a while an officer who spoke a little English would try to interrogate us."

Larry spoke of this progressive severity of punishment from his Korean captors as well. His group was starting a death march of their own from Manpo on October 31, 1950.

Larry said, "Up ahead, the guards were making sport of the weaker POWs. They took turns kicking the stragglers in the rear, laughing and jumping up and down as they did so. They were not yet using their rifle butts to beat the prisoners over the head; that would come later when this first game was no longer considered fun. But at the moment, any hapless POW who lagged behind the main group was considered fair game by the guards."

Larry was traveling under the command of a North Korean commander known as the "Tiger." He was soon to see him personally shoot a prisoner, Lt. Cordus H. Thornton of Longview, Texas. Lieutenant Thornton's offense was that some of his men had been too ill to keep up with the death march's pace.

Under the Tiger's leadership, cruelty was rapidly learned. Both Mickey and Larry agreed that the North Koreans were, in general, worse in the treatment of prisoners than were the Chinese. The difference in death and life blurred in both.

Mickey continued, "For a while they held the POW group at Kangge, Pyuktong, and near Pyongyang. They finally settled us in POW Camp 1 at Changsong. We watched a lot of dogfights, heard their stupid lectures, and tried to stay sane and alive.

"I do believe that willful, deliberate neglect killed most POWs in North Korea while we suffered through brainwashing studies. The horrors of being a POW in Korea was watching friends die from disease and wounds. The lice, flies, and rats ate on us as we endured illness and starvation. Still, the other was worse."

Mickey paused, changed the subject, "Talk about brave and guys to admire, those navy corpsmen attached to marine outfits, nobody knows how many of us they kept alive over the next two years. Maybe it'd just be something simple like, 'If you're going to eat that, let's see it gets ground up good.' Of course, they had no medicine, but they've got my gratitude for their diagnosis and advice."

I have yet to meet a combat marine who did not pay tribute with respect, admiration, and gratitude to the navy corpsman. These sailors were assigned to marine units as their medical support. Their tracks marked where others died or suffered, and they were placed there in the midst of battle. They exposed themselves to save others. Some objected to killing. All objected to dying.

Mickey continued, "And the British, you talk about team-work and humor. Some Yanks had different opinions of them, but they were up to something all the time, always helping each other and harassing the enemy."

Larry spoke of the courage of the Irish and English by high-lighting their eternal struggle with one another. In doing so he conveyed the futility of the North Korean prison hospitals. Rarely did prisoners escape a visit to them alive.

He detailed the death of three prisoners, priests, in less than three weeks. "The second, Father Frank Canavan, as he was being led away to the hospital for the second time, turned around, waved his hand, and shouted, 'This is nothing. You should have seen what the English did to the Irish!'"

Larry did not overlook praising his French comrades' cour-age. "Father Joseph Cadars stood up, threw back his shoulders, and called to Father Joseph Bulteau in a surprisingly loud voice. 'Father Bulteau, how does a French soldier die?' The reply came in a thin, crackling voice, 'Bravely, Father, bravely.'

"This dialogue was repeated each morning until Father Cadars died on December 18. Father Bulteau died on January 6, 1951, leaving only Father Coyos of the original six French priests. A Frenchman can cry without having to account for it to anyone; he can also die bravely."

Mickey switched from his comrade's bravery to the ever-present hunger and the battle of minds. "About all we had to eat was the propaganda they fed us constantly. Those commissars acted like evangelistic crusaders at twenty-four-hour camp meetings, piping that dogmatic communist stuff at us. I just tried to stay quiet and think survival while keeping my mouth shut. We tried to work together for the common good. I studied Chinese and Japanese during idle time.

"Usually we'd get a little something to eat twice a day, but we seldom got water. You'd start going night blind and they'd bring in a cartload of carrots. Everybody would have carrots for a while then that'd play out and you'd start going blind again. They brought seaweed, kelp, I think it was called, anyway it was supposed to be high in iodine, vitamins, and good for thyroid goiters. Other than that it was generally a little rice, maize, millet, corn, barley, and rotten potatoes every once in a while. Sometimes we'd get fish. No telling how long some of that fish had been dead before it got to us. Most food was either rotten, wormy, dirty, or all of the above."

Larry Zellers also mentioned the effects of poor diet. "I suffered from night blindness during our second and third winters in captivity. It's caused by insufficient vitamin A. The condition could vary from simple "tunnel vision," where I could see only a small circle, to total darkness; when it was very bad, I could not see anything at night, even with a full moon. When we were taken anywhere in the winter at night, I had to be led by the hand. The total calories in our rations at Ujang had been more than sufficient, but the diet was still not balanced. Later, with good food and a proper diet, it disappeared. It never returned."

Mickey said, "We were held at POW Camp 1, Changsong, not far from the Yalu. There we watched dogfights between the U.N. and Chinese or Russian fighter planes. We were bombed several times at night. The camps were not marked with Red Cross insignias."

Nick Tosques, a member of the 555th Field Artillery Battalion, was captured by the Chinese on April 25, 1951. He arrived at Camp 1 at Changsong, near Mickey, approaching the end of June.

In Rudy Tomedi's *No Bugles, No Drums*, Nick spoke of the high altitude jet dogfights. Likely he and Mickey observed some of the same air war. "One thing that cheered us up was the dogfights. Our camp was only a few miles from the Yalu River, right under MiG Alley, and we could see the MiGs and our jets fighting almost every day. They were too high for us to see which planes were which, but one day they brought in a captured pilot, and he told us to listen to the rate of fire. The MiGs had a slower rate. After that we'd cheer like hell every time a MiG got shot down.

Chapter
11

Crowded Foxholes
and Curb Service

I left the guys at Ward 111 in late February of 1952. I clung to my stubbornness to the bitter end and disregarded Dad's advice by volunteering the fourth time to continue active duty. The orthopedic doctor handling my case gave me a final examination of the broken leg.

"Murdock," he said, "this break is as good as it's likely to get. It could be used as a crutch to defer military service or we can send you on to boot camp. I think you'll make it okay, but I can't promise it won't lock up on you at sometime in the future. What'll it be?"

I told him I was ready to get it over with. My orders were cut sending me on to finish boot camp the following day. In early May of 1952 I reported aboard the LST-1146 at the San Diego, California Destroyer Base.

Like most of the world, the crew of the LST-1146 ate well while the POWs suffered through starvation and diet deficiency. Aboard ship, lack of fresh produce and dairy products were a minor irritation on long stints at sea and soon gave way to powdered milk and eggs when on our annual expedition to the Arctic, but the rest of the time our meals compared to those of civilians.

In contrast to combat or POW existence, our only food shortages were pretty much self-generated. If memory serves, our longest voyages without re-supply were only in the range of a few months. Still, we often left Seattle with the main deck jammed with extra refrigerators and the fantail piled high with sacks of potatoes stacked to the bottom of the gun tubs and covering the size of a small garage. Planning was sufficient so that any shortages we experienced should be of short duration.

Unfortunately those calculations failed to allow for the sheer lack of discipline of my mates and me, the 1146's crew. Potatoes, when quartered, make excellent missiles for anyone interested in chunking at sea gulls. By the time we were at sea far enough to get away from the gulls, the potato pile on the fantail would always be greatly diminished.

After the stored food supply had been exhausted in the above manner and the monotony of sea duty grew, the next raid for food items was often directed at the lifeboats. Emergency supplies there always failed to last until the Aleutian Islands were reached. Our rationalization had to do with making the theft less onerous because reality said one could hardly last long enough in an open raft on frigid water to get hungry anyway. The only way to approximate the ignorance of those committing such acts is to multiply by two the intelligence of the officer corps that allowed it.

Dallas native Kenneth Wilkinson served in the marines and saw action in both the Pusan and Inchon areas of Korea. He was in A Company 5th Marine Regiment 1st Brigade. His outfit moved a short distance inland and then sometime later Kenneth returned with a number of buddies to the beach area to sneak a quiet lunch. He mentioned pock-marked beaches, shot-up warehouses, and nearby stranded U.S. Navy LSTs. By the time they were able to take a moment for a meal, thousands of men and dozens of tanks and other vehicles had passed through the area.

"I noticed stacks of rice against one of the buildings. It was only a few feet from where we worked at our rations. One of the guys walked over to the sacks. He carried a cup of coffee, freshly heated. The cup spilled when he set it on one of the bags. From a few feet below came a clipped shout of pain. There was a damn machine gun nest of North Koreans there."

(FX3-Aug. 5) HEADED FOR THE FRONT—U.S. Marines march from the dock area of a South Korean port on their way to trains that will carry them to the fighting front after their arrival on Aug. 2. (AP Wire Photo) (echo7105md) 1950
Photo courtesy of Kenneth Wilkinson

Chapter 11

(FX2-Aug. 5) HONOR GUARD GREETS MARINES—An honor guard of
five Koreans with flags of the Korean Republic, United Nations,
and United States, followed by a mixed band of U.S. Army
and South Korean musicians, greets the first shipload of
U.S. Marines on their arrival at a South Korean port on Aug. 2.
(AP Wire Photo) (echo7105md) 1950
Photo courtesy of Kenneth Wilkinson

"They were right in the middle of the landing forces and
knew they were dead if they gave themselves away by firing,
huh?" I questioned.

"Yeah, but they might as well have made a stand, they
ended the same way," Wilkinson said.

Glen Thompson was assigned to a machine gun platoon
when he arrived in Korea as a replacement in early 1953. He
spent the first night on the front alone, manning the .30-cal.
weapon. Soon another soldier was assigned to keep him company. "We were not compatible," Glen said. Even to this day

Thompson has shoulders like a bull. I can't imagine anyone doing anything but agreeing with him.

"We couldn't decide who was the gunner and who was the assistant.

"Besides that, he would drive you nuts. Things would be perfectly quiet and he'd say, 'You hear that?'

"He'd call up to the C.P., 'Hey, we got incoming down here.' Maybe we'd had nothing come in for hours. He kept me uptight. I couldn't get rid of him though. We were together a long time."

Boiled eggs and pickled pig's feet at a bar in Saginaw, Texas, after the war brought back memories of foxhole hunger and discomfort to an ex-army friend. He was only a few months back from Korea. We had driven over from Denton. He said, "Man, I remember a time in Korea these would have looked good. We'd been pinned in our holes for hours, taking mortar fire. Occasionally they'd take a short break in the firing, but about the time you stuck your head out, they'd start again. This went on and on. Sometimes the lull would last longer than other times. I got hungry then passed that to weak and worn out then on to a point I didn't give a rip. Finally we got another few minutes of quiet."

Some guy at the shuffleboard behind us yelled, and the ex-soldier flinched then continued. "I decided, to hell with it, I might as well get blown apart as starve to death. I removed my helmet, shook the dirt out of my hair, put the helmet back on, and stood. I smoked a cigarette, waiting to see if the peace would hold, trying to get my courage up to step out of that hole and make my way down to the kitchen several hundred yards away.

"Finally, I started walking. I'd gone a few yards when, kiss-my-ass if this guy didn't stick his head out of his hole and holler at me.

"'Going to the kitchen?' he asks.

"'Yeah,' says I.

"'Bring me a sandwich,' he says, 'any kind will do.'

"He's lucky I didn't shoot him. There I was, scared to death, starving, and this cowardly son of a bitch asks me to bring him a sandwich."

"What'd you say?" I asked.

"Ain't sure, but he got the message."

I pondered whether to mention dining on lifeboat survival rations. I decided against it. I started to tell about searching the North Pacific for a mail buoy my first trip up but decided to wait for a lighter moment for that one also. My stories just didn't seem very heavy. We ordered another round.

Short Men—High Water

Hall laughed. He'd just beaten me arm wrestling. No one else in the ward would challenge him. There were a couple of others who might have, but fortunately for us, their wounds were to the arms or upper body. Arm wrestling was restricted to guys with leg injuries. Our arena consisted of two wheelchairs with a bed stand lowered to elbow height between us. You could face the chairs in opposite directions and compete with right or left arms. We'd lock the wheels and go at it.

Finished, we stored the chairs at the end of the ward, got our canes, and joined a group at the bedside of a navy corpsman. This guy's name is lost in faded memory, but he'd accidentally shot himself and messed up both hips while fooling with a .45 automatic. His cast was from his waist to his knees. A brace was plastered into the cast on both legs. The thing kept his hips immobilized. At the time of his injury he'd been assigned to marines in Korea. Now Pruitt and another guy chatted with him.

"How you feeling, Doc?" Hall asked as he took a seat. "When they gonna get you a gurney to row around on like the goldbrick's got?"

I looked and saw the goldbrick at the far end of the hall.

"Feeling well, they said next week maybe. How about you, getting any movement in that knee?"

"Can't complain." Hall shook his head and fished for a cigarette. The conversation slowed to a halt. Lieutenant Honeys rushed past and waved a clipboard at one of our group, a marine sitting on the next bunk. The bunk was empty. The marine stood, found a chair, and smoothed the wrinkled blanket on the bed.

"Hall, tell Doc about the first time you called for a corpsman," Pruitt said.

Hall looked at the bedridden sailor and laughed. "Heard it?"

"Don't seem possible, but don't think so. What happened?"

Hall took a drag of his smoke. "It 'uz the first time I was under fire. We were advancing up this hill when the gooks started lobbing some fairly heavy stuff at us. We hit the deck. I remember my face buried in the ground, and I'm trying to get lower. Some of that stuff is coming in pretty close and we're getting jarred around.

"Pretty soon, I smell something burning then all of a sudden I get this sharp, fiery pain in my back. Oh, God! I'm hit, is the first thing comes to mind. I holler, 'Corpsman, corpsman, help, I'm hit.'"

"Well this corpsman rushes over. He's bent down and moving out when he gets to me. He sprawls there beside me and hollers, 'Where?'"

"Right between the shoulders," I holler.

"Well, he starts slapping around back there then jerks my pack off. He takes out his canteen and pours about a half-cup of water on me then rolls me back over pretty rough."

"'You'll live,' he grunts and bends low, rushing to someone else.

"'How bad am I?' I holler.

"'Just a hot fragment burned through your fatigues. You got a blister the size of a match head,' he hollers back. You talk about embarrassed."

"A chopper evacuated you when you got that knee busted up, didn't it?" the corpsman asked.

"After a couple of ROK [Republic of Korea] boys got me off the hill. That was pretty damn scary."

"How so?" I asked.

"At that time, those guys had itchy feet. Some had been known to bug out. Anyway, earlier, my weapon, a BAR, jammed on me. I was working with it when that thing hit my leg. Man! I rolled over on my back and somehow my leg goes up in the air. It goes on past straight up then bends at the knee—the wrong way. My toes almost hit me in the mouth.

"Well, they got something tied to it and one of the guys tried to bandage it some. They wrapped the whole thing in a poncho and sent me down that hill on a stretcher with these two South Koreans carrying me. I could sense blood sloshing inside that thing all the way down. Even later lashed to that helicopter, I could feel it.

"Going down the hill, we hadn't gone far when these two boys carrying me started jabbering in Korean. They pointed. On the ridgeline not far away figures moved around. They were well within range. It was enemy troops, no doubt about it.

"The Koreans stooped to put me down. I think they said, 'We stop, hide.'

"'No, no, we go on. Not the enemy, friends, the British, English troops! They are friends,' I knew if those guys ever set me down they were gone and I was there to stay. From the amount of blood in that poncho, I didn't have a lot of time to wait around. I don't know if they believed me or not, but they got me off that hill."

Hall's story is pulled from memory and clouded by fifty years time. But recently Staff Sergeant Hardie Lee Richards confirmed the wisdom in Hall's fear of being abandoned. He told of his own uneasiness concerning the dependability of South Korean porters that made a similar trip with him. Richards was with the 1st Marine Division, Howe Co., 3rd Battalion, 7th Regiment.

He said, "We used labor battalions of South Koreans to carry supplies up to the lines during the spring offensive of 1951. We were somewhere in South Korea and meeting stiff Chinese resistance on May 31st. That was the day I got hit. We were taking a lot of incoming, heavy mortar [120mm] fire. They were also raking us with Russian-made machine guns. We were pinned down. We took a lot of casualties."

In our phone interviews in 2001, Hardie Lee's voice seemed little changed since I'd known him in Ward 111, fifty years earlier. He'd agreed that as long as the book told the truth, he didn't mind passing on his story. As he discussed the actual event, I thought I sensed tightness in his voice. "What hit you, shrapnel or a bullet?" I asked.

"A mortar fragment, I guess. It entered the shoulder, blew away a couple of inches of collarbone and went on down into the lung then exited through my back. There's an artery there near that collarbone. I don't know how it missed that. Looking back, it seems a wonder I didn't bleed to death. Anyway I slumped over a machine gun the guys were using. I guess they tried to move me so they could continue firing."

"'Move, Sergeant!,' one said.

"'I can't move,' I answered.

"They must have tossed me out of that hole, out of the way. That's all they had time for. I don't remember much about it, not even the corpsman who got to me and dragged me over to

How Co., 3rd BN, 7 marines machine gun squad in Korea
(L to R: Bauman, Cherry, Richards, Rhodenbough, and Sheaffer)
Photo courtesy of Hardie Richards

the reverse slope of that ridge. I got to shake that man's hand for the first time a few weeks ago [2001] at our reunion over in St. Louise; Charles Hughes is his name. He treated me as best he could, saved my life then put me in the hands of South Koreans to be carried down the hill to an evacuation point."

Navy corpsman Charles "Doc" Hughes responded to my question over the phone in late August 2001. "Richards, Richards, yeah, chest wound, yes, I remember Hardie Richards. Sure, Mackey, come on over; I'm glad you're going to get the story out. We had guys down all over that hill the day Richards got it." I thought, how fitting—his memory of the wound then the name.

Doc Hughes is now Doctor Hughes, Professor Emeritus of English at Henderson State University, Arkadelphia, Arkansas. A few days after our phone conversation, we spent several hours together in his home. He made dozens of pages of personal writing concerning Korea available to me.

He wrote of the afternoon Hardie Richards was wounded and his own outfit's effort to make its way up to the ridge. He and his buddies called it "The Crag."

"The assault began on Memorial Day, May 31, 1951. First, second, and third platoons leapfrogged through each other. The third led off, reached their objective, and stopped. We moved through them then the first moved up and passed through us. They soon disappeared into the stunted trees, and the silence fell again, more intense than before. We waited. As the seconds passed, my hope began to rise. Maybe the enemy had fled. Perhaps the artillery and the air strike and the sight of hundreds of charging marines had done the job.

"The mountain had completely swallowed up the first platoon. It was as if they had walked off a bottomless cliff. Only faint pecking of rifle fire from one of the distant ridges broke the painful silence.

"Suddenly the quiet was shattered by the single blast of a burp gun. It sounded very loud and very close. A second passed. The burp gun ripped again and was answered by three punching reports from a rifle. The whole ridge above us exploded with small-arms fire. The noise swept the mountain with inordinate fury.

"We did not move. Overhead, ugly bits of steel sang through the sky. The lieutenant shouted into the walkie-talkie. We hugged the ground and waited.

"A marine emerged from the trees to our front and scrambled toward us. 'You got a corpsman? We need him! Send him up!' He turned and disappeared into the trees.

"'There you go, Doc!' someone shouted to me. I rose stiffly and started forward.

"'Be careful, Doc.'

"'Yeah, we need you, Doc.'

"'You don't have to worry about me,' my voice cracked.

"I advanced up the mountain in a crouch. A ridge swelled before me. The roar of battle pressed in on me, but I seemed to be alone on the mountain. I scrambled over the rise and found myself in a depression of the ridge, a "saddle," perhaps thirty yards long. I saw the first platoon. They occupied a line of positions on the far rise. Trenches and spotted foxholes crisscrossed the saddle, which offered some protection from the hail of fire. Through the trees, on a flat scar of earth, I saw the first platoon corpsman bending over a wounded marine. Five or six others lay alongside. I ran to them.

"'Which one?' I asked, breathing hard.

"'That one over there. Better see about him.' He indicated one of the prostrate men with a nod of his head. I later learned this was Hardie. I bent over the wounded man and spoke into his chalky face. He was barely conscious. I ripped away his blood soaked shirt and exposed a tiny maroon hole about two inches below his nipple. With each gasping breath bright red blood bubbled from the hole and flecked the deathly white of his skin. I scratched through my bag and found a roll of tape and sealed the hole. I turned him over and sealed a slightly larger hole on his back. Then I laid him on his wounded side and squirted a syrette of morphine in his arm.

"My platoon moved up and reinforced the men in the trenches along the rise. The battle continued without letup. The din was painful to the ear. Bullets whined. I tried to shrink myself, to make myself small as I worked."

I am sure he did try to make himself small on that ridge in Korea. Instead he made himself tower tall in the eyes of his marine buddies. Today he lives on another hill, but this one has a swimming pool just off the patio.

★ ★ ★

Richards continued on the subject of his evacuation and Korean stretcher-bearers. "I remember we came to this stream. It ran swift and was pretty deep, and these Korean guys carrying me were shorter than hell. I mean little. I thought, there's no way these guys can keep me above that water. I'm gonna drown before I can bleed to death. They'll drop me for sure; but they didn't."

I mentioned Hall's fear of being left behind by his South Korean stretcher-bearers.

"Yeah," Hardie Lee said. "At that time they moved out pretty quick when trouble started."

"I recall you telling of having a rough night before you were evacuated," I said.

"Uh-huh, I got to the evacuation point too late for the last flight back to an aid station. There were several of us. One fellow died there that night." Hardie Lee changed the subject, asked for my phone number, then added, "After you called the other day, I got to thinking. We called you 'The Kid,' didn't we?"

I laughed, "Probably. Tell you for sure, I'd answer to that today. I'll soon be seventy."

Anybody Here From
Charlie Company?

In June of 2001 Staff Sergeant Hardie Lee Richards filled in
some of the blanks in my memory. We talked by phone—him in
Idaho Falls, Idaho, me in Garland, Texas.

"Collins," he said. "The guy with the ruined elbow was Collins. I don't remember his first name."

"Did he pitch in the minor leagues for Oklahoma City?" I
asked.

"I don't think so. That was another guy. It's possible there
were two minor league pitchers, but I don't remember Collins
being a ball player. I remember this other guy being pretty
upset at his career in baseball being wiped out. Best I can recall,
you got the rest of it right."

I sat near Collins' bunk when the following incident
unfolded in Ward 111, late in 1951. The goldbrick and several
marines were in the group with me. Collins lay in his bunk. A

marine from another ward walked to the edge of our group. He was a new arrival to Corpus, just back from the Far East. He wore pajamas and slippers. I never knew his rating, and his name escapes me. For convenience it'll be Jack. I'll never forget the event.

The new arrival waited for a pause in the conversation then spoke. "They tell me some of you guys were in Charlie Co. 3-5 [fiction]. I'm trying to find out about a buddy of mine. He got it in early May. I'll be seeing his folks. They'll want to know more than I got. Any of you guys from that outfit? Thought I might find somebody who knew him, you know, learn how it happened. Understand y'all got a guy from that outfit." Jack ground out his cigarette in an ashtray one of the men held.

Collins wore a half-cast on his right arm. The plaster had obviously been formed around the arm then the upper half cut away from the wrist to the top. It was held to the arm by bandages and the whole thing rested on a pillow. Discoloration showed on the wrappings at the elbow. "That'd be me, _____ Collins. Have a seat. What did you say his name was?"

"Elliot!"

"Uh-huh." Collins' eyes seemed to fade and his lips tightened ever so slightly. One of the seated marines scraped his chair. I heard a breath escape from another. I lit a cigarette and looked back at Collins.

His face blanched; a muscle twitched in his jaw then his lean features hardened. He glanced jerkily, left then right. The cards Collins had just been dealt would test the best poker face. His features that had been so blank a moment earlier, now had it all written there, the agony of loss, the bewilderment of living while others died.

One of the marines, maybe Hardie Lee, Bobby Don, or possibly Pruitt, held out a light to Collins' cigarette, but he waved it off and flicked his own Zippo to life. He nodded toward his right arm. "They say it's screwed up forever." He avoided eye contact, gazing into the distance. You could sense the energy the man used in his struggle for self-control.

"Tell you what, Collins. I'll come over tomorrow, and we'll have a cup of coffee and talk about it," said the new man.

"No, Jack, let me tell you. He'd want you to know."

I stood. "Here, have a seat." The stranger stepped a couple of feet toward the goldbrick and lit a smoke.

He took the offered seat. He glanced at the window. It was opened as high as it would go. He wiped sweat from his forehead on the back of his left arm. He waited. He watched smoke curl from Collins' cigarette, then the words he hunted but obviously didn't want to hear came at him.

"We were friends." Collins said. "Anyway, you know about what it was like over there then. We didn't get hit too hard until the day before. Old Elliot took a hit in the thigh, a million-dollar wound. You know, no bone, just a lot of meat and a ticket home." Collins managed to wash the expression from his face again. Only an occasional twitch hinted at his agony.

"Soon things eased up some, and me and this corporal got a chance to try and get Elliott on to an aid station. We 'uz afraid he'd bleed to death. We picked up some help on the way down. The others had his feet and I cradled his head with my right arm." Collins crushed the smoke in an ashtray balanced on the sheet stretched between his legs. He flicked ash from his fingers and tugged slightly at the pillow his arm rested on.

"I guess the damn gooks had that area zeroed-in because the first thing I knew, I caught this thing through the elbow that went right through Elliot's head. He never knew what hit him."

One of the men coughed, stood, and motioned to another in our group, and they moved away. Jack continued to sit, staring at the clenched fist in his lap.

It seemed there should be more. I examined the overhead, lowered my head, and traced the pattern of the floor tile, wondering.

Collins shook cigarettes partially out of his pack. He extended them toward the newcomer.

Jack nodded. "Collins, the information, I appreciate it." He stood, pointing at the bandaged elbow. "Hope that does okay."

The coincidence of these two men coming together in this fashion, with the catalyst of a dead companion binding their destiny, lived with me as a sort of rejected or partly repressed memory. In rare moments and later years I told others, always thinking Collins' loss was compounded by the fact that he'd been a professional pitcher before the war. The sadness of that memory is true, but the players in the lineup are perhaps different.

However, Hardie Lee Richards wrapped up the improbability of the moment during our discussion fifty years later by adding an additional coincidence to the story. His voice came strong over the phone. "Yes, Mackey, I remember Elliot was the one Collins was carrying."

He said, "I, too, had known Elliot. I knew him before Korea and was in the general area when he was killed. I'd not known Collins until we got to Ward 111 and did not know of his connection with Elliot. However, while in Korea, I'd heard Elliot lost his life and went to check. I raised the poncho they placed over his face and verified his identity over there.

"I was pretty jarred that day when Collins told the story. I later visited Elliot's family out in Plainview, near Lubbock, told them all I knew.

"I'll tell you another time I was surprised. Do you remember Bernard Hopper? He had a leg that was stiff like Hall's."

"Yeah, I remember him. He was from Vera, also, wasn't he?" (Vera had a population of about two or three hundred.)

"Uh-huh. He and I went to high school together. I didn't even know he was in the marines until he hobbled into Ward 111 one morning."

Bernard Hopper (left) and Hardie L. Richards
Photo courtesy of H.L. Richards

"Wasn't he the guy that used to tell about helping his father capture rattlesnakes then send them to Florida to be milked to produce antivenin shots."

"That's the one. His leg was a little different from Hall's. I think his bullet sort of bounced around, but it left it stiff like Bobby Don's. I wouldn't know how to tell you to get in touch with him. He had a sister named Maxine that went to school there in Vera."

To this point I've not located Hopper. I'll keep trying.

The casualties recuperating in Ward 111 received toothpaste and shaving items routinely from Red Cross workers who visited the wards. Earlier on New Year's Eve, 1952, the more ambulatory guys had primped with Red Cross items from their ditty bags before hitting the beach. By dark things in the ward were pretty quiet. Generally, only the more recently or seriously wounded and those confined to bed or wheelchairs remained. My reason for being aboard had more to do with being broke. I'd not earned months of piled up back pay to spend.

About the time most of the guys got out of sight and the quiet had began to squeak, relief appeared. The Red Cross arrived with an over-the-hill piano player and a stripper who'd crossed that same high ground a number of times. A couple of little old ladies, no doubt from the local chapter, and an important-looking fat man escorted them. Tonight the troops would be entertained. There would be no more long faces. Nothing was too good for America's fighting men.

This was indeed the home of fighting men, but most who saw this entourage streaming in wanted to run. I, in particular, could sense this night would be "beyond the call."

Naturally, the battlefield veterans pointed at me, "The Kid," caught the stripper's eye, and commanded, "Sic 'em!" It was a fate I'd have had to fight for had the lady been younger, shapelier, or in dimmer light. With palpitating breath the ancient vaudeville escapee performed her out-of-step bump-and-grind routine while looking up and over her shoulder into the farm-boy face of the only recruit in a thousand miles.

The anguished melody of her companion's off-key and out-of-tune notes accompanied my debut. I almost literally fulfilled the old show business line of "break a leg," with my good limb entangled in my walking stick and the other confined to a cast. Later I vowed to never hesitate in accepting free Red Cross toiletries in the future. My account was balanced for life.

Of course liquor was not allowed in the ward, but earlier in the day a marine received a late arriving Christmas package that had followed him across the Pacific to Korea and ultimately arrived in Ward 111. It contained a case of maraschino cherries packed in bourbon-filled bottles. The case quickly disappeared, except for the last bottle. Somehow it found its way, as a present, to the desk of Lieutenant Honeys, nurse on duty.

Chapter
14

The Best and Worst of Duty

John O'Callaghan from Irving, Texas, missed our cherry fla-vored party in Corpus Christi on New Year's Eve 1951-52. John traces his Irish American ancestry back to County Cork, Ire-land. Family legend has it that a fourteen-year-old ancestor stowed away on a ship bound from Liverpool to the United States. From that humble beginning John grew to be an optimist and anticipated enjoying a change of luck and pulling some good duty in the state of Nevada in 1953.

"We were stationed in Pendelton at the time. We'd done some fire fighting, trained a lot, and I'd been down at Camp Elliot Rifle Range instructing in rifle training some. Boring stuff, you know. Man I couldn't believe it when they came through and told us to get our stuff together. We were going to Nevada to pull guard duty at some test sites. They issued us live ammunition. Now, here was the good part: we'd pull four days guard duty then have three days off in Las Vegas before going back to the field.

"They flew us out there in Sikorsky helicopters, and it was all they said it would be—three days in Vegas every week. I never bought a meal or paid for a drink all the time I was there. There were only four hotels then: the Dunes, the Desert Inn, maybe the Sahara, and I don't know, it could have been the Flamingo.

"I'd go to the nickel slots. If I hit a good streak, I'd go over to the crap tables. Boy I hit a streak once. I was rolling for a dollar a whack. I couldn't miss. This guy came up wearing a sports coat. He had both pockets stuffed with hundred-dollar bills.

"He said, 'Man, I'm gonna go with you.'

"I made four or five passes in a row. Then I got this feeling. I turned to the guy betting on me and said, 'Let's both get out.' We did and sure enough the next roll I crapped."

"He said, 'You saved me money, here take this.' He handed me a hundred-dollar bill. I'd never owned one before. I later saw that guy cash a check for ten thousand dollars. I got no idea of his identity.

"But I came down to earth from all that pretty quick when they started setting off the A-bombs around us. That's right, the tests were atomic. Yeah, they lit off—that's what they'd call it, 'light off,'—the first four tests ten to fifteen miles away, then they lit off the fifth and last one two and a half miles from us. They had this 300-foot tower built of 14-inch-wide girders. The devices (they didn't call them bombs) were placed atop the tower and set off."

We talked at John's kitchen table in Irving forty-eight years after his experience. "Where were you guys when those things were going off?" I asked.

"The first, the ones at ten miles or so, we'd be patrolling the perimeter. When they were ready to light it off we'd get the word, and they'd have us go up on this ridge to watch. We were in a six-foot-deep trench we'd dug when the last one was lit. They told us to look down when the blast occurred. You talk

Cpl. John O'Callaghan (entering from right) boarding a helicopter for transportation to Nevada nuclear test sites in 1953.
Photo courtesy of John O'Callaghan

about bright! There were others in that hole with us—scientists, civilians.

"If you ever see an A-bomb the light is what is different. And that last one, so close, its light was different. It was so bright there were no shadows in that six-foot ditch. It was the brightest thing you ever saw and hope to never see again."

"You say it was different from the others."

"Yes, there were three sequences of this high intensity light. Between each would be a slight dimming then a new brightness, maybe six to ten seconds in length. The first four were like, maybe, just a single flash, and we'd watch, like I say, from the ridgeline, but that last one, man, that was something. I looked up, maybe that cloud of smoke and yellow flame was 3,000 feet up, just a great big round ball with a blue aura of radiation, reacting with the gases in the air, I guess."

"It wasn't mushroom shaped, then?"

"Maybe, to someone out a distance away, but not underneath it like we were."

"How long before you got out of that trench?"

"Maybe ten to fifteen minutes. They had us come up and board a helicopter. You know, when we came out of the trench, desert cactus that had been green before the test was barbecued as black as anything you ever saw. They carried us to the tower, ground zero. That tower was vaporized. They had poured a slab of concrete I don't know how thick, feet maybe, for the tower to sit on. When we got there, the slab was gone and where it had been was this great big concave hole with concrete turned to gravel or sand."

"And what kind of protective clothing did you wear?"

"Nothing. The only thing they ever did was once a week for three weeks, they ran a Geiger counter across the heels of our combat boots to see if they could detect excessive radiation in the cobbler nails."

"I'd think you're a lucky man, John O'Callaghan! You've never had any health problems due to radiation sickness?"

"Nothing I'm aware of. I've lost track of the rest of the men. Don't know about them. There were about thirty of us."

"Were you guys uneasy about being exposed to those things?"

"Naw, it offered a change of scenery. Didn't seem like much of a deal back then. But I did get scared once. On that last one, after the lights and fire all died down some, there was just this big old cloud formed. There was a breeze pushing it. That thing was drifting straight for Las Vegas. Really, straight for it, and it wasn't too far away."

★ ★ ★

Few military men got stationed near Vegas. During the days of Korea, any bull session on good duty ultimately turned to

Japan. Most of the servicemen I knew spent time there. I missed it. I want that on the record. This is all hearsay.

During the Korean War, Japan had a reputation—a good reputation. So good, we'll do away with identity while we discuss it.

The men who live wars try hard to understand them. Talk the subject and they will tell you it's ugly, maybe bad. They avoid the heavy rhetoric of writers and politicians and grow uncomfortable with terms like honor, courage, sacrifice, hero, and hallowed ground. Few mention its loneliness.

Yet its cost on relationships, young love, and families is only slightly less disastrous than the physical wounds. War may or may not be a normal human condition. Gender separation is not. Both have grave consequences.

In *Trails Ploughed Under* Charles M. Russell wrote of entertainment sought at trails end: "Married men don't like history too near to home." Shipmates and fellow servicemen spoke glowingly of their time there, and many returned with symptoms of "Asian Fever" often contracted beyond the date line.

Warriors of the First World War probably were not the earliest to immortalize the choicer duty found behind the lines of death by singing their "First Marine" ballad. "The first marine went over the top, parlez vous...the second...the third marine he stayed behind to kiss the ladies and drink the wine, inky-dinky parlez vous."

Japan was a staging area for Korea. Battle weary army and marine fighters returned there for R & R. Sailors and airmen were in and out frequently. Far from America, exotic, beautiful in its own right, and recovering from the ravages of being conquered, all the pleasures of the world were packaged there for the United Nations serviceman with a few dollars and time to spend it ashore.

The gentle nudging of a ship at its moorings, the monotony of soft oriental music filtering beyond dim lights and through the shadows of the harbors hinted at the pleasures ashore in Japan. For a man on liberty, pictures and keepsakes had little meaning in a world where every ounce of energy was directed at avoiding all thought of tomorrow. Such a world's nebulous nature demands physical contact.

If the music, the setting, the sounds promised make-believe or oblivion, a couple of drinks and the sight of soft skin, tiny waists, and gentle curves of the fragile beauties of this oriental island added to and kept the promise. They proved more companionable than many American servicemen could soon forget. To married and single men alike the pledge of "Me no butterfly" was urgently solicited. On rare occasion it lasted a lifetime for both parties. More often a lonely soldier or sailor only added a greater burden of grief and guilt to his already miserable role.

Married men suffered worst from this malady. Its symptoms were easily confused with other emotional trauma and called for hours of space staring, best performed from high bunks into low overheads and of slouching around for months with little energy. Venting general dissatisfaction with everything and everyone semi-civilized seemed to offer relief. In its critical stage some fathers and husbands were so enchanted with their Japanese girlfriends that they wished to abandon stateside wives and children and spend eternity bobbing before the colorful glow of an oriental lantern. A few nautical knots of a ship's wake pointing to a setting sun served to cure most, however.

★ ★ ★

Captain Clarence Archer flew transports, had his wife with him in the Mediterranean and European theatre during most of the Korean War, and still found a way to get into trouble at home. He found himself stationed in Tripoli, Libya, and spent a lot of time setting down air force transports on just about every piece of blown out desert hardpan on the North African coastline. Remote radar sites required regular air support. Trips to

Turkey, Iraq, Iran, Greece, Saudi Arabia, and Casablanca made up most of his destinations.

The mention of good duty causing strained marriages brought a grin to Archer's face. He spoke of pulling a weekend assignment as base adjutant at his home base of Tripoli one weekend. He foresaw no sign of storm clouds.

Among the duty adjutant's responsibilities was the resolution of traffic ticket violations on the base. It takes little imagination to understand the consternation Archer must have experienced when his wife entered with a speeding violation of a 10-mph zone. He had to serve as judge at his wife's court appearance.

★ ★ ★

Wadie Moore mentioned, "I pulled a stretch of duty in Korea as the company's radioman. Before long I'm toting a radio with a six-foot antenna. I think they gave me the thing because I was too small for anything heavier. I'm thinking man, good duty. I learned fast, not so! In combat that is not something you want to be doing. That thing sticking up like that draws a lot of fire."

Hell on a Hill

Sergeant Wadie Moore's experience with being abandoned by South Koreans validated the others' concerns about the responsibility of their Korean allies; still, he thinks their action may have saved his life. "We, the U.N., issued South Korean civilian workers blue coveralls. These Blue Boys, as they were known, had me wrapped in a poncho and were transporting me across a river after I'd been hit. I couldn't see, but I could hear this swift running water, hear those guys splashing and grunting, trying to tote me across that thing. Then we came under mortar fire. A second later I'm dumped in ice cold water."

We were in the Moore's living room in Commerce, Texas. Mrs. Moore, Norma Jean, shared the visit with Wadie and me. She spoke quietly, "Their lack of discipline, perhaps, saved my husband's life. Doctors later told him the cold conditions of the river's water and the subsequent, frigid chopper evacuation may have lowered his body temperature enough to promote blood coagulation and thus increased his chances of survival. He'd lost a tremendous amount of blood."

After failing the Marine Corps minimum weight limit on his first try, Wadie Moore stuffed himself with bananas and water. He returned hours later with a bursting bladder and a couple of ounces of weight to spare. He made the weight. The date was December 5, 1951. He departed for Korea aboard the transport ship the *General William Weigel* a few months later.

I'd entered the home of Mr. and Mrs. Moore at their invitation and after they'd learned of my old friendship with Staff Sergeant Richards. They knew each other through marine reunions. I had explained my mission and read a few notes I'd prepared for the book. I stopped with "I'd like to listen for a while."

Wadie sat erect, eager, drinking coffee. He spoke with emotion and precise detail. It was easy to imagine the months, years in hospitals he'd spent reliving his experiences. He

Wadie Moore (in uniform) and Hardie L. Richards
at 1st Marine Div. Reunion in San Diego, California.
Photo courtesy of Hardie Richards

wanted them before the world. They were too enormous for one mind and body. He wanted the world to share. Of that I'm confident.

"In early May 1951 we arrived in Pusan, Korea, unprotected, alone, ill clothed, ill fed, and ill prepared. I saw no brilliant marine minds at work. What I saw was a bunch of junk, officers and noncoms that were fat, soft from peacetime service with minds as thick as cork. That bull about the marines as superior this, that, and the other...bull. What we had was a bunch of men and boys thrown together, each with a spark of individual greatness buried deep inside them. We were there for cannon fodder, sent to plug holes, expendable, available to buy time for the U.N. to fight a war. We became all those things the marines like to promote, but it came from within, from what we brought with us into the corps, not from some special toddy served in boot camp.

"I remember being overcome by a feeling of, you're not going to make it out of here. From Pusan we flew by DC-3 to Pohang airstrip then trucked north about twenty-six miles. Another guy and I stood in back of a six-by leaning over the hood talking. Artillery fire cracked around us. We looked at each other. 'I think this is war,' he said.

"A little later we pulled over and let some guys come down, going the other way. They were used up, looked at us with disgust and contempt.

"'Where's the war,' I hollered.

"'Don't worry, sweetheart, you're going to find it,' this guy replied.

"The guy was right. Soon the bodies, the stench was unbearable. I know a marine uniform when I see it, and some of those bodies were marines. War was no longer abstract, and I'm vomiting on that truck."

Wadie gathered his emotions then smiled. "The dead weren't the only ones that smelled. We went into this staging area, Charlie Co. was down on the right close to Baker. Fox was on the left. Next morning I joined my outfit and found myself looking up at the worst smelling, most obscene guy in the world, Gunnery Sergeant Speill. I mean this guy still had eggs from boot camp on his shirt. I can hear him to this day hollering, 'Where's my little buddy? Moore, get your rabbit-ass up here.'

"We saw some tough times together and he proved himself over and over. He knew how to fight a war.

"Henry Montabono of George Co. took part in a pretty good firefight with Sergeant Speill. Henry is barely five feet standing on tiptoes and is from Meraux, Louisiana. In the middle of this thing, the sergeant grabs Henry and says, 'Hey Shorty, don't you know they are trying to kill you? Stay behind this tree. You see something, shoot at it.'

"A few minutes later the Gunny looks at Henry and says, 'Shorty, you'd better get out from under that helmet or else the corps is going to court-martial you for desertion.'

"Shortly after that Staff Sergeant Joe Mickey "Whiskey" Finn becomes sort of a mentor to me. He gets me assigned as a runner for the company commander. He sort of looks out for me because of my size, I guess. Gets me off of some of the heavy muscle stuff. First thing I know, I'm running around saying the company commander wants this, said that."

Norma Jean took Wadie's cup and brought him a glass of juice. I declined and stayed with water. Moore continued. "Two months later it was August 1st, and we fought a number of enemies: stifling heat, water shortage one week and monsoons the next, heat and dust, insects, vermin, and shortages of ammunition. Really there were times we had nothing to fight with but to hit 'em with the butt of our M-1s. We were still an army of thieves, fat cats, and cripples.

"It was about this time I met this old man, twenty-five-year-old Staff Sergeant James Dettman. He was a forward observer, and I learned to love that man. He comes by one day and says, 'Wanna go snoop and poop?' Now being a forward observer is not the smartest thing in the world, but this guy was intelligent, intuitive, and just knew how to get the job done.

"I said, 'Sure.'

"He said, 'Bring a carbine and nothing that rattles, and come on.'

"I did, and we go out two or three miles beyond the front lines. James is reading leaves, smelling around, and every once in a while looking at his compass. We come to a raised area, nothing that stands out, just a little knoll with brush.

"He says, 'This looks like a good place to rest.'

"Well, we settle in there. Down below is a stream, and by it is a little shotgun hut. A cow grazes on lush grass a short distance away. Things are quiet and we see no movement for the longest. After awhile two men come out, turn their backs to each other, and take a whiz. They go back in and soon a few men drift in and enter the hut.

"This goes on most of the afternoon, and after awhile those two men have become one hundred. Well, old James takes out his compass and map and figures his azimuth for that hut and calls back to George battery. He gives them the numbers and then says, 'Give me three round of H. E. and fire for effect.' Seconds later those rounds come in and that hut and those hundred or so men have disappeared. The old cow is still grazing out in the grass. That cow is more used to war than any human I ever saw.

"When James and I get back to the front line, I get the word, 'Moore, it's your time to go on patrol.' Nobody likes patrol. You always have some guy that's trigger-happy with you. It's quiet and dark and spooky out there. This night we hear a movement in a bush and our bunch fire over forty-eight rounds into that thing. A moment later this silhouette appears against the sky with it hands reaching up and we hear, 'To-shong, to-shong'

[surrender in Korean]. Well, this guy has only a half-inch scratch on his right butt, and that just goes to show, all marines are not crack shots."

Moore adjusted his glasses over the patch that covers his right eye. He took a drink of juice. "After that our next objective was a ring of mountains north of the 38th parallel and six to ten miles from where we were bivouacked, up to our ass in mud and water. We stopped awhile at the Soyang River, on its eastern bank. To ford it we grasped hands to cross as a human chain. You know, tall men on either end, and short guys like me in the middle. We got to the center of that thing, and in ten minutes it had gone from hip to shoulder high on our tall guys and my feet are floating out in front. That water was swift. Our line broke and half a dozen guys were swept downriver.

"I saw this guy come running down the bank of that river like crazy. He bailed off into that water. It was Ed DeFlice, and he'd pull one guy out then do it again. He saved two or three guys then George Williams did the same thing and got three or four more. Those two really did a job. They got Bronze Stars. We had two, I believe, drown.

"We got ourselves back together then, some on one side, others on the opposite. About this time some smart officer comes up with the brilliant idea of getting some ducks up there to cross on. The Skipper had a bottle of Seagram-7 and he rationed out a shot to each guy. Dwight Young it was. After several attempts to contact him in his hometown of Phoenix, Arizona, we learned of his death from a reliable source.

"Before we got to those mountains I learned you can walk while you sleep—I did it. We crossed a shallow river about daylight one morning and there was our objective. The high ground overlooking supply lines made it valuable. The army called it 'Heartbreak Ridge.' We knew it as Hill 607, Kanmubong Ridge at the Punch Bowl.

"We fanned out to move up fingers of this mountain of 30 to 35 degrees. We moved carefully. When we were about halfway up, the shit hit the fan. James Dettmen and I were together. We took everything, 81mm mortars, burp guns, .50-caliber machine guns—every bit of it. Small arms, you name it! When someone tells me what hell's like, I've been there. Sheets of dirt, rock, and tree fragments rained upon us. We had gooks all around. There was only one thing to do—fight forward or fight backward.

"Dettman and I hit this depression together. I look out, right into the mouth of this machine gun. The gunner is trying to take me out. James and I pooled our resources and put ourselves back to back. We were in a crossfire. Anyway you moved they were going to get you. The water jacket on the .50-caliber trying to get me looked big as a saucer. If I could hit that thing, the barrel's heat would make it sway down out of commission in no time. For the moment the depression is shielding us. The .50-caliber's fire is bouncing off and over us by inches. Then I realize there are some ammo-carriers I need to get. While I take out that machine gun, Dettman keeps 'em off our ass and talks to F-80 Saber jet pilots providing air support.

"'Do you think we can get out an air panel [markers to guide the dropping of napalm]?' Dettman hollers.

"Well we get the marker out and aircraft make their run. The world turns to fire, and we are scorching. We'd been engaged since about 7:30 or 8:00 A.M., and it's now 1:30 P.M. or so.

"I'm getting hotter then something hits me. 'Oh my God! I'm hit!'

"James looks at me. 'You're hit bad.'

"I felt the depression in my head where my eye used to be. I could see nothing. My nose was gone. I can't see!

"'A piece of what hit you hit me,' James said. 'Wadie you're hurt bad. You've got to do what I say. I'm gonna give you some instructions. You gotta do exactly what I say.'

"I didn't lose consciousness and wasn't scared. I prayed.

"Dettman said, 'Can you crawl forward one yard then back one yard to your right? You got to stay on your belly, squirm. After you go a yard to your right crawl forward again until you feel yourself falling, belly on the ground, keep going.'

"I did it, blind, squirming along, all hell overhead. I couldn't see anything then I heard this strong black voice, 'Get that man in here. Get that marine in here!' It was Doc Willie Stewart, navy corpsman, and he packed the cavity in my cranium and gave me a vial of morphine.

"'Wrap him in a poncho,' Doc said. Then it was bumpity-bump-bump down that hill with somebody dragging me in that poncho. Oh, it was cold! Surely this ride will be over soon. Then we came to this stream and the communists were throwing mortars into that thing until you'd think they were going to blast all the water out of it."

After being dropped and abandoned by his Blue Boy porters, Moore heard the sergeant directing the helicopter evacuation of wounded holler, "Get that man floating downriver —get him!" Marines dragged him to the side of the water and soon he was strapped in a basket whizzing through the air on the 90-mile trip back to adequate hospital care for the seriously wounded.

"In those days the choppers were so frail they had to have a dummy for ballast opposite the wounded. It wasn't necessary in this case as my old friend Ed DeFlice served that purpose. We shared the coldest ride of our lives."

Those Who Serve

War is not something sane people choose. Still, there are a number of reasons for doing your duty once immersed in its madness. In all walks of life the tendency is to look for shortcuts and the easy way. The world abounds in those who are capable of rationalizing two plus two into five when given enough incentive. When alternatives involve life or death, how can one say with certainty how he will respond?

Some serve nobly, others search for less than honorable ways to avoid years of low pay and difficult assignments or worse. Feigned illness is one of the favorite methods of avoiding service.

Military medical personnel are aware of this tactic. They watch closely for such cases. They are especially sensitive to complaints that are difficult to verify. Back pain is typical. Try as hard as the medics may, the fraud often wins. However, in wartime the medical people often demand their pound of flesh before capitulating.

A sailor prowled the corridors of Ward 111 in 1951 wearing a body cast from chin to toe. He complained of unconfirmed back pains. When I met him, he had worn the plaster for three months. He moved about on a wheeled gurney. For propulsion this wearer of a plaster-of-paris turtleneck used walking sticks in either hand and, belly down on the wheeled bed, moved about the corridors. A towel covered the essential body function openings.

The southern Gulf Coast of Texas is warm and humid most of the winter. Body plaster and humidity are a bad combination. If being disabled from scratching an itch earned medals, the guy just mentioned would have been too heavy to move. No one, neither staff nor crew, shunned him, still no one offered to push him around either.

At the end of six months recuperation, I waved bye to the "goldbrick" on my way to further duty. The back patient had a few more months to go before being cut free.

★ ★ ★

When the enemy draws near and gunfire rumbles, some shoot themselves in the foot—literally. I awoke one morning to find the bunk next to me, vacant the night before, now held a patient. The young man was a marine fresh off the line in Korea. His wound was through the top of his right instep. A half-cast supported and immobilized the injury. It still drained onto the lightly taped gauze that covered it. The private seemed pleasant and lacked the hurt and shocked expression carried by many new arrivals from the front lines. This guy seemed almost happy with his current plight. He explained by a twist of fate the bullet had missed all bones.

Later in the day other marines validated my suspicion. My new bunkmate had a self-inflicted wound. Like the gurney rider, this poor man was pretty much left to entertain himself. No one confronted or obviously shunned him, still he was sort of semi-ignored. It was as if all knew that "there, but by the grace of God, goes I." Even those with grievous wounds seemed to acknowledge that next time or the next they, too, might crack and do the same. I remained cordial to this new arrival while hoping I never faced the dilemma that so marked this man, one bunk down. With time I observed the young man's pleasure turn to sadness. Some wounds hide beneath the surface.

Sergeant Wadie Moore mentioned going to investigate a single gunshot in Korea. It was not long after a firefight during August 1951. This was a short time before he saw action at the Punch Bowl in Korea. "We hear this single shot off in the bushes, and like a streak we are on our way to check it out. When we get there we see this marine stretched on his back. Blood is running out of his boot. His rifle is pointed in the general direction of his foot. He had his ticket home."

Was it the same guy I later met in Corpus. Who knows? The timing was right, but those guys had lots of company.

Wadie had said earlier, "My motive when I joined the Marine Corps on December 5, 1950, was not to kill anyone; I wasn't mad at anybody. Patriotism never occurred to me. I had one desire. That was to escape degradation and poverty. I mean clapboard, two-room, chicken house kind of poverty."

A moment later Wadie had another thought. "When I was deciding what branch to go into, I was just a green kid and I'd noticed those girls seemed to follow those blue uniforms around."

My personal vote is for Wadie's second thought. I remember how much attention Gene Kelly got from my high school dates with those bellbottomed navy trousers when he danced across the screen. I've already mentioned a desire to sleep in clean beds as a reason for opting for the navy over perhaps another branch. The main reason of course was that I thought I had a better chance of avoiding getting shot.

Bud Archer jumped for the military while fresh out of high school in 1943. He wanted a chance to learn to fly. He'd already written Piper Aircraft Company to receive a free plane flight. Hooked on its thrill, fighting a couple of wars seemed a cheap price for a life pushing those things around the sky.

John O'Callaghan said he chose three years in the marines over four in the navy or air force. His alternative was a pending draft notice, three weeks away.

"My high school buddies and I talked each other into dropping out and joining the marines in 1947," Kenneth L. Wilkinson said.

Wounded in Korea, even today the ex-marine leaves little doubt that he's a scrapper. I interviewed him in 2001 in Carrollton, Texas. I thought I detected a bit of disdain on his part a time or two when he mentioned officers. Like many enlisted men he seemed to retain a little discomfort with the idea of the privilege of rank. Still, at least one officer in Korea discovered a reason to be proud to have such a man as Kenneth Wilkinson on his team.

"Before I got hit the last time, we came under fire one day and scrambled for shelter. Still in the open an officer went down in front of me. I drug him to a corpsman. I don't know his name. He likely would have done the same for me.

"But another time we had this 90-day wonder. He didn't know from nothing. He was dangerous. I remember a 2nd lieutenant who liked to have several men in front of him at all times. I'm not kidding. This man wanted three men covering him while he bathed."

I'm glad our country has men like Kenneth Wilkinson. I have no clue how a man walks in front of a tank attempting to locate land mines while on a road last traveled by the enemy. He earned two Purple Hearts doing that sort of thing. I'm glad we're on the same side. It's not infrequent to find those who rankle most under discipline often prove themselves in deadly combat.

I asked Wilkinson if given back the years he'd change anything about going to war. I wasn't surprised at his reply.

"Somebody had to do it."

Did any of us think of the plight of the Korean people? I think not. Neither the power-merchants pulling the strings nor the kids sent to pay the price gave a rip about a nation they'd never heard of. The Domino Theory was the prevailing political view. The belief was publicized that each country that fell brought bearers of destruction closer to the front doors of Americans. Fight them over there or see your loved ones fight them at home. Was that a consideration? Probably, yes, though less than bellbottom trousers, three squares, or dress blues.

Navy corpsman Charles Hughes, assigned to H Company, 7th Marine Regiment, spoke of a campaign against guerrillas west of Pohang during January-February 1951. "We continued for another four hours, stopping periodically for the officers to compare their thoughts of where we were. Mostly new replacements, we were not yet toughened to the field and were exhausted by the time we were told to scatter on the ridgeline and take up positions for the night.

"The sky was clear and cold and the moon, almost full, already high in the eastern sky. With my entrenching tool I had just scraped a place for my sleeping bag on a piece of rocky ground when I heard the first burst of gunfire I ever heard in actual combat. It was not directed at us but came from the valley below. I dropped my shovel and moved to a better vantage. I could see the glowing trajectories of the tracers as they laced through the darkness below.

"As I watched the tracers, I experienced a revelation. Too young for World War II, I had grown up on John Wayne and William Bendix war movies and had felt cheated that I had missed that war. Here at the age of nineteen I was provided an

Charles "Doc" Hughes
Korea 1951

Olympian view of the folly of man. Below me were two groups of men intent on killing each other! It was the sheer reality that awed me now, that reality that can never be captured in pictures or words. My weeks of combat training had not prepared me for this. For the first time I realized the significance of what I had done when I volunteered for duty with the fleet marine force."

Mickey Scott said he'd always wanted to be a marine. That was perhaps the biggest incentive—the bombardment of propaganda we had all received as teenagers throughout the Second World War. Mickey also said, "The G.I. Bill was important to me."

Economics did play a big part for all of us. We came from a generation of kids that in general knew what work was about and how tough a dollar could be to come by. Certainly the three of us I mentioned who decided to leave college and join the Navy thought of the possibility of returning on the G.I. Bill (we did just that).

Veterans like Sergeant Hardie Richards, Captain Bud Archer, and others called in from reserve and guard units were all playing an economic card in being in those organizations, but they didn't flinch when it came time to belly up to the bar and pay their dues on active duty.

The bulk of the guys who served were drafted, but they all knew the way to Mexico or Canada. They went, maybe not willingly, perhaps unhappily, but in general ready to fulfill an obligation. Did they "bitch"? I never met a serviceman who wasn't good at it. Were we different from our younger brothers in Vietnam? I doubt it. What about our older brothers who served in WW II? I don't think we were a lot different.

Why didn't we try harder to avoid going into the service? I believe one reason is that most remembered the shame and disgrace heaped by the community on those who dodged the draft during World War II. Even a future potential draftee's motives in having a child brought scorn that went beyond the father to the baby. "Weather stripping" was the snickered name, the connection being to keep one out of the draft.

Men lost contracts on sharecrop farms or posh jobs because they turned up 4-F, medically unfit. The rumor followed them the rest of their life that they somehow elevated their blood pressure by taking various over-the-counter drugs or deliberately failed the eye test. Sons of draft board members were scrutinized day and night. Many a bloody nose and possibly even shootings resulted from relatives of servicemen meting out their own form of justice to some who stayed behind.

The Long Road Back

Frequently words not spoken by veterans sound louder than the stories they tell. Norma Jean Moore, wife of Sergeant Wadie Moore of the marines, spoke quietly as the three of us sat in their living room at Commerce, Texas. The sergeant had just finished telling of how ill prepared and supplied his outfit was in Korea during mid-1951.

"They were forced to scavenge to stay alive," his wife said.

A few minutes later Wadie added, "We were still an army of thieves, fat cats, and cripples." He never elaborated on the thievery, and I did not pick up on it. My judgment is he'd been forced into more than just midnight requisitions.

Retired teacher and ex-marine Marvin Dunn lost a foot and a portion of his leg in Korea. He invited me to his home for an interview. "You know," he said after discussing his experiences for a couple of hours, "we have very close friends we see routinely. He and I were both in Korea, near each other, but for thirty years we never mentioned any part of it. There may as well not have been a war. We talked of everything else. Not many years ago one of us asked the other something about it, and now we rehash it frequently.

"I do have to admit, though, that even my best buddy who was with me when I got hit can't tell me much about it. I asked him not long ago, and he said, 'I don't know. I knew you were hurt bad, and I was so afraid for you that I haven't a clue what hit you.'

"I couldn't see at the time, but I remember hearing him fussing at those Korean Yoo-boos that were going to tote me out of there. He didn't think they were taking good enough care of me."

"How do you spell Yoo-boos?" I asked.

"I don't know, but that's what we called them."

Perhaps the worst casualties of war are not those found in graves. It might not be the ones missing in action. Some live

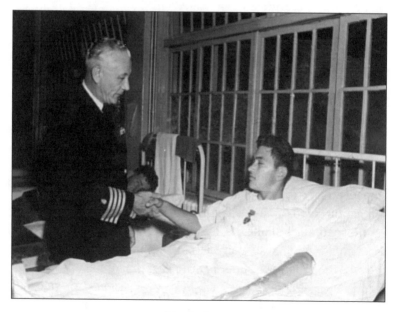

Marvin Dunn
Photo courtesy of Marvin Dunn

but never make it back all the way or if they do it is with heavy baggage. Often a piece of them remains behind. Call what they leave on the field innocence, childhood, perhaps humor, or all of the above. Too often that loss is replaced with anxiety, guilt, and trauma. War reaps more of a price on some than on others.

Perhaps one discovers on the battlefield that circumstance often rules over will and precludes choice and performance, making the world a lonely place. For some the lapse of hope, ambition, and human emotion becomes the reward wrested from the garbage of war. Often these scars heal more slowly than the physical ones.

Sergeant Ed Miller of the 11th Marine Regiment was evacuated due to injury before reaching Hungnam on the way down from the Chosin Reservoir. He volunteered to go back to Korea after five days in a hospital and thirty-two days of R & R in Japan. He later became the third man to rotate back to the States from his battalion. He said, "On the ship coming home I conducted a song service on deck each night. Somehow, that led to me becoming sort of an unofficial counselor for others' emotional problems." Ed's return voyage occurred in June of 1951. The prior year had not been pleasant.

Physical rehabilitation takes many forms. Staff Sergeant Hardy Lee Richards worked hours, week after week at the exercise room at Corpus Naval Air Station Hospital. The challenge he had was to improve the mobility of his arm and shoulder. His primary machine was a simple, solid wooden wheel about two feet in diameter with a swiveling handle. The wheel turned or spun on a central pivot or axle. It looked a little crude by today's standards, but it was prescribed by his doctors. Richards worked at his task faithfully.

All the men with ankle, knee, or leg injuries who had recoverable joint movement worked on various bicycle-type machines or strength building leg exercises. Bobby Don Hall of Marshall had a stiff knee beyond recovery. He worked diligently on the rest of his body to maintain fitness to compensate for the disability.

Larry Zellers returned from years in a North Korean prison camp a shadow of his former physical self. He witnessed the most base human behavior mankind has to offer. Spiritually, however, he had a mission. He pursued that mission through the seminary and as a chaplain in the United States Air Force ministered to young servicemen and their families throughout his career.

Mickey Scott returned from his Chinese POW camp, in his words, infected with nearly every known ailment. He spoke of a year's time of belligerence and doing nothing. By the time he returned to college, he apparently was ready to buckle down.

My ex-GI friends and I in college after the war certainly did little to distinguish ourselves as student role models. Of course, my bunch had done little better prior to Korea. I recall the same being true of the single World War II veterans who returned to my hometown after that conflict. Their drinking, rolling in the streets, brawling, and shooting craps kept my generation of teenagers entertained for several months. I'm afraid we mimicked their behavior only too well.

Wadie Moore spoke of recovery, of rousing from his chopper trip after arriving at the hospital. "There were lights shining on my face. I looked up at these people over me and asked, 'Am I gonna make it?'

"'We can't tell you,' was all they would say. There was a Catholic priest and a Jewish rabbi leaning over me with the doctors.

"I guess it was sometime after that I woke with the worst pain I ever experienced. It was my combat boots. They were still on and shrunk from all that river water. You talk about hurting."

Moore was flown to Yokosuka, Japan, then later on to the army hospital at Tripler army base in Honolulu. Later he was flown to Oakland Naval Hospital, California.

"There I met a young navy surgeon, Commander Joseph R. Connelly," Wadie said. "I was seriously wounded, emotionally traumatized, and my life was going to hell if he didn't turn it around.

"The first thing he did was remove my bandages and poke a mirror in front of me. 'Look at what you're going to live with the rest of your life.'

"My eye was gone. There was a hole in my head, and there was little left of my nose."

"'Yes, you're deformed, but you must remember there are others worse. I want you to promise me you'll never let another doctor work on you. I'm the best in the world, believe it. I'm gonna fix you up, but you'll never be pretty, and we're gonna be together a long, long time.'

"Time followed one operation to the next, and Christmas of 1951 approached. I asked to go home for the holidays.

"'No,' he said. 'You're not able. Besides you're still too damn ugly.'

"I insisted and finally he relented.

"'Okay' he said, 'but no drinking, carousing around, or any of that kind of stuff.'

"Well, the greatest thing of my life was back there. She had been this little ole kid when I left. Someone I never paid attention to. Wow, was I shocked! Norma Jean Henderson, the most beautiful girl in the world, sweet, and she acted like she liked me.

"I told her I was going to send her an engagement ring when I got back to base.

"They told me when I returned to the hospital that Commander Connelly had taken a couple of weeks leave and then was to transfer to Bethesda Naval Hospital, Maryland. I went ballistic.

"'Wait,' they said, 'there's a letter for you on his desk.' The letter said to pick up my orders. I was being transferred to follow him.

"At Bethesda I told the commander I wanted to get married.

"He said, 'No, you can't. What is a cripple like you going to do with a wife? You are still too ugly.'

"I wrote her and told her we would have to wait a bit. She misunderstood and sent the ring back. We were married October 23, 1952.

"Three years I was under that doctor's care, and then it came time to part. He asked me what I wanted to do. I said, 'Surely the marines can use a cripple somewhere in an outfit of this size. Commander, don't let them discharge me.'

"'Wadie,' he said, 'you can't stay in. You're crippled too bad.'

"That man never failed me. He called a captain over in records somewhere. He said, 'Captain, I got a man here who needs to be medically retired, not discharged. Can we do it?' He looked at me, 'You'll have over twice as much income, a lot more benefits, okay?'

"They did it, retired me as a buck sergeant. In 1954 we settled in Commerce. I later got my Ph.D."

Wadie and Jean have two children, Kevin and Quinn. A friend, the president of the college, had visited with them the previous evening. Honor and tradition play a big role in developing America's young people at Texas A&M and its branch campuses. They are fortunate to have a couple such as Wadie and Jean on their faculty representing those ideals.

It's a long way from Commerce, Texas, to Kodiak, Alaska, and even further in time since I last saw my old ship the USS 1146, still, it seems like yesterday. For a vessel that could only churn up fourteen or so knots at flank speed the USS LST-1146's wake followed her over a lot of sea and ocean. I served aboard her from shortly after leaving the hospital until the end of the war. Her squawk box alerted us to "no-drill" general quarters on a few occasions and announced the armistice to all hands somewhere in the Bering Sea in July 1953. It was the sweetest sound I heard her communicate. (Those same boxes had told other sailors of VE and VJ Days.)

The ship had ferried troops around Korean waters in the early days of the fighting of 1950, then participated in the Inchon invasion in September of that year. She cracked amidships during a typhoon while a part of a convoy adjacent to

North of the Arctic Circle—Mackey Murdock (left) and Bill McGill (right) pose near an outbuilding at Barter Island, Alaska in Aug. of 1952. The building is native. Nearby is the radar.

Korean waters. In addition to longitudinal reinforcement for ice at the waterline, she wore that storm's scar in the form of a fifteen-inch by half-inch steel band-aid welded transversely around her amidships when I reported aboard in May 1952.

Bill McGill reminded me in 2001 that he was aboard when the typhoon caught the LST-1146 and cracked her amidships. They weren't on their way back from Japan as I had thought.

"We were on our way to Korea, in the Sea of Japan. Mackey, we were taking 36- to 37-degree rolls. You know that's about all you can stand on one of those old tubs. We obtained permission to break formation and turn into the waves. Then we had seas breaking totally over us.

"After Inchon, we ended up going back to the shipyards in Yokohama. Good welding always fascinated me, and the Japanese welder that did most of the welding on that thing was the best. He told me he learned the trade during the war working on ships our guys had shot up."

Marine Sergeant Ed Miller heard me mention serving on an LST. He spoke of traveling from Japan to Korea on one manned primarily by Japanese just prior to landing in Inchon. "Out on the Sea of Japan there somewhere, we ran into this typhoon. It was rough. I think we lost an LST from our group in that thing."

Hopefully, the one he missed was the 1146. I mentioned that was likely the case and if so she made it on into Korea then safely to the States.

I bid goodbye to the old bucket and my shipmates at Kodiak harbor in September 1953 and caught a MATS plane back to the lower forty-eight for discharge from active duty. My reserve strategy had paid off and saved me a couple of years of peacetime service.

Petty Officer Second Class Morningstar raised from his bunk and shook hands on that day forty-nine years ago. He bade me goodbye. He pulled his watch from his wrist. "Here Murdock, I owe you five dollars." I had forgotten the debt.

Turning my back on my two-year home brought mixed emotions. I left a lot of friends aboard. She looked like what she was, moored there to the dock in Kodiak, an old workhorse.

Mountains come down to the harbor. A form of tundra, some kind of Alaskan grass, grew lush upon them in the summer. The green-capped, sheer bluffs exposed silt. I remember the wind blew and swirled little wisps of sand high on these ridges.

The harbor was clean, the water deep blue. The sun shone, and my ship and my mates and the Good Lord above had seen me safely through the war. I'd been given a few decades to fulfill other destinies before meeting those heroes Pruitt spoke of, the ones who did not come home. No more Ward 111, no physical evaluation board for me, man, how lucky can you get?

Arctic DEW and
Metallic Pings

T he early fifties were fraught with peril. The North Koreans crossed the 38th parallel, the Communist Chinese the Yalu River, both with guns blazing. Unverified at the time, Russian and American airmen frequently engaged each other in dogfights of supersonic aerial warfare over North Korean skies. Even today, mystery shrouds armed conflicts that may or may not have occurred between the Soviet Union and United Nation's warships.

On July 28, 1951, 1st Class Petty Officer Bill Mackey served as electrician mate aboard the USS *Ulvert M. Moore* (DE-442). His ship steamed in waters off Korea's west coast in the Yellow Sea. Their mission, along with the USS *Renshaw* (DDE-449) and four other destroyers, was to provide screening support for two light carriers, the HMS *Glory* and the USS *Sicily* (CVE-118). The task element's objective was to maintain air superiority and control of events on the ground all along the western sector of North Korea from the 38th parallel to the Han River.

Negotiations had begun at Kaesong eighteen days earlier. Some cards were on the table. Others were yet to be played. The U.N. wanted the Soviet Union, the Communist Chinese, and the North Koreans to understand that our side was ready and able to strike at will into North Korea. Did the Soviet Union send submarines into the Yellow Sea to harass this and other similar missions? Were they prepared to torpedo ships of the United Nations command?

Allison E. March and Donald C. McElfresh have spent a number of years researching these questions. They have no definitive answer. They do have a book, *Submarine or Phantom Target?*, detailing their work. On page three they state, "Suddenly, at 1913 [7:13 P.M.] July 28, 1951, the *Renshaw*, on a base course of 135 degrees true in station #5 and at a speed of 15 knots, reported a sonar contact to the Task Element (TE 95.11). The contact showed to be on a bearing of 026 degrees true bearing and at a distance of 800 yards. The Task Element Commander, Captain Thach, ordered the *Renshaw* to proceed to overtake the contact and to attack it as an unidentified submarine. The USS *Ulvert M. Moore* was detached to assist the *Renshaw* in the then accepted manner of attacking an unidentified sonar contact thought to be a submarine."

March and McElfresh's research, interviews, and study of ship's logs support that the two destroyers made a number of depth charge runs and "expended a significant amount of their ASW [antisubmarine warfare] arsenal" in their two-hour attack before being relieved by other ships. The relief ships continued to attack the target and remained in the area for many hours.

Sonar men of the *Renshaw* gathered and compared notes within minutes of returning to normal "Condition 111." They were justifiably excited by the frantic attack they had participated in. "Each wanted to relive his perceptions of the events that had just transpired. They agreed upon their identification of the contact as metallic, underway, and at different depths. At other times it appeared likely to be lying on the bottom during their attack. An oil slick was observed by their crew and later by the ships that followed them into the attack."

Shortly afterward while these men were comparing notes, "An officer came down to sonar from the bridge and without any discussion went to the sonar log and with a pair of scissors cut all pages out that described the attack they had just participated in. The sonar log was a hard cover, bound book of legal size, and they could see the edges of the pages sticking out from the binding. The log had at least two or three pages with information on the attack, ranges, Doppler angles, depths, and time. The officer's attitude at the time that he was removing these detailed records of the attack was, 'Forget it, it didn't happen.'"

I spent a lot of time with my old friend Bill Mackey before Korea and afterward. As a matter of fact he supported me in making one of my better decisions. He performed "best man" duties at my wedding. He'd never mentioned the incident of his ship's attack on a possible Russian submarine until I contacted him in 2001. He sent me the book with markers at his quotes. I thought I knew all of his war stories from both wars, but I'd missed this one.

I'd learned in early 1952 that Bill's ship suffered a fatal casualty from a Korean shore battery. I read the story in the *Stars and Stripes*. At the time I pulled galley duty at Great Lakes, Illinois, awaiting orders to the fleet. It was a short article, and I read it a second time while pushing a smoke break into a third cigarette. This was long after the "phantom sub" attack.

March and McElfresh's book quotes Bill as follows. "My memory of that time involves a lot of depth charges—many of them too shallow and too close, and those of us in the engine spaces thought we were going to blow ourselves out of the water.

"I also remember watching from a topside vantage point while the *Renshaw* dropped depth charges. Rumors? Some said it was a Russian submarine—others said, 'there was nothing there.' Still others swore they saw an oil slick, but I don't remember seeing anything like that. There were also those who speculated it was one of our subs and we probably scared the hell out of them. Bottom line, I don't remember anything worth repeating."

Later, Bill responded to another query from March and McElfresh: "I am sure the officers of the *Moore* at the time had far more knowledge than was ever divulged to any of the enlisted men aboard."

Like the enlisted men of the *Moore*, there was a lot going on aboard my ship that I wasn't privy to. In the summer of 1952, we scrambled to General Quarters Battle Stations in the Bering Straits between Alaska's Seward Peninsula and the Siberian coastline at the Arctic Circle. The squawk box's last phrase was, "This is no drill."

We loaded with live ammunition and waited nervously for a target. My battle station was the aft 40mm gun tub, and my job was to pass the clip of rounds to the sailor loading the gun. The armament of LSTs of that period was twin 40mms fore and aft and 20mm and .50-caliber mounts amidships on both sides of the vessel.

Distance between geographic points in that area is normally generous, but at the Straits, the Soviet Union and the United States are closer than kissing cousins. In the winter a day's sled ride on the ice can transport locals from one nation to the other.

On the morning I mentioned, fog hung heavy about us above a calm sea and the temperature was cool, in the low 30s. Several minutes later, a Russian ship broke through the fog bank, towering above us. It was a freighter of some type gliding

Author Mackey Murdock aboard the USS -1146
at Treasure Island, California.

almost silently through the sea. She approached within a hundred yards of our port bow. So far as we knew we weren't at war with the USSR, but if memory is correct, we were aware that they had shot down a United States plane a few weeks earlier. The plane was supposedly farther from their shore than our position at the time.

129

To my knowledge, no sign of recognition or greeting passed between the ships, and the incident amounted to no more than a little tense breathing on our part. Did I see weapons on the freighter? No. Are 40mms adequate for such a foe? No. Could she have rammed us with little damage to her hull? Yes, but our cargo of aviation gasoline, diesel oil, dynamite, and live ammunition would have created problems for both ships.

I saw and heard a lot of gunnery practice rattle that old amphibious tub. That ship near Siberia presented the only target I ever felt we could not have missed. She was almost on top of us.

The battle of nerves between the two giant superpowers was not restricted to ocean activity. It included the skies over the homelands of both countries. On either side of the North Pole giant bombers sat poised, armed with nuclear warheads for the heartland of the two countries. The shortest and least detectable route to the U.S. led directly over the Arctic. If one chose to listen, he could almost hear the tick of the clock toward a showdown. The players had elevated "High Noon" to a monstrous level.

The free world needed a hi-tech edge. Something to alert its nations that the enemy was en route. That something, a giant radar network, was created and installed by scientists and military personnel. It was called Defense Early Warning (DEW). Between the pole and the Arctic Circle on our continent, it was cooperatively placed in an arched line on northernmost land areas of the North American continent and others of the free world.

Supplying the outpost created a unique problem. The sites were in the dark more than half the year, and the temperatures were among the coldest in the world. Runways had a way of disappearing in the soft tundra in the summer and twenty feet under snow in the winter. There was an ocean at the doorstep of each site, but it was frozen up to the beach for three hundred and forty-five days each year. The navy concentrated on those fifteen to twenty open days. That was the window. It opened in late July or early August, a sliver of free water a few yards wide from the beach to the ice pack running from Pt. Barrow east across northern Canada.

Getting a ship through this free water might have been a piece of cake except that the water along the shoreline was shallow, too shallow for all ocean-going ships except the ugliest of all. The amphibious scows known as LSTs seemed to fill the need best. Two were earmarked from the fleet to have a strip of reinforcement buffeting plate welded around their waterline to reduce the possibility of ice puncturing their skin. The LST-1146 was one of these two vessels. The number of our sister ship escapes me.

Much of the lighter cargo for the DEW stations was carried by bush pilots and smaller cargo planes. As mentioned earlier our cargo consisted mostly of diesel oil, aviation gasoline, ammunition, dynamite, and a few snow vehicles. The dynamite was for the U.D.T. (frogmen) to use in blasting passage through ice fields and to free the ship in case of entrapment. It was hoped the ammunition would not be needed, as the Soviet Union was the only likely adversary in those waters.

Tex's Shooting War

"Wanta hear my one shooting war story?" old shipmate Charles Arthur "Tex" Owens asked.

We had just finished catching up on forty-eight years of being out of touch by condensing the events of those years into fifteen minutes of "Son-of-a-gun, I wouldn't have known yuh" at his kitchen table in Longview, Texas. Labor Day 2001 had just slipped by.

"That's what I used to call it when the kids were little and wanted a little entertainment, 'My one shooting war story.'"

In keeping with our early training, the thought of romance took precedence over shooting, so we were a while getting back to Tex's thought. He mentioned a friend marrying a girl who had a good-looking cousin. The "looker's" name was Lillie Maude Allen. The cousin was embarrassed by the lack of height on the guy she was seeing. This occurred in 1951. The match-maker explained to the other lass that she knew a guy who had

"Tex" Owens aboard the LST-1146.
Photo courtesy of Tex Owens

a nose longer than the beau in question. Tex brushed his generous muzzle as he warmed to our conversation.

At six-foot-three he had apparently passed Maude's muster on that long ago first date. The day we talked she excused herself to go check on their vacationing kids' pets. Amusement showed in her face and she smiled closing the door.

Her car engine sounded outside. "I wrote her when I got back aboard ship and asked her to marry me. She answered back immediately with a yes.

"I got permission to see the Old Man. When I told him I had a few days on the books and wanted time off to go back to Texas and take care of personal business, he looked at me like I was crazy."

"'Why didn't you take care of this while you were on leave, son? You've only been back a couple of weeks. We got men on board...'

"'I know, sir. But you've got to put me in the brig or let me go home—I wanna get married. If I go on liberty I ain't turning around until I get to Texas.'"

Later Tex admitted to a second rebellion against the strict discipline that so chaffed us all. "You were aboard when we broached 'broadside-to' out there on the strands of Coronado."

I nodded.

"We came listing into dry dock, under tow, three days later. You know, I thought I might have overstepped it a little with an officer out there, too," he said.

The incident he spoke of was one I'll never forget. We had almost lost the ship and did for all practical purposes make a complete wreck of her. She was in dry dock for months getting fitted with a new hull from the starboard waterline to the same mark on the port.

"Yeah," I recalled, "I was striking for damage control. I worked under Manau. He and the exec were in water, fighting to shore up a rupture in the skin of the starboard shaft alley

135

entrance nearly all that first night. Hypothermia set in and they were forced to their sack for a while. The first thing I knew I had the deck force assigned to me for damage control. The way I remember it the Old Man dropped that stern anchor too soon."

"No," Tex said. "He dropped the anchor too late and then it couldn't get enough of a bite to hold. When the bow hit the beach, those swells just pushed her broadside too."

"I'll be damned. Tice was on the fantail. I thought he said they dropped too soon then lost cable and everything. Anyway, what was your deal with the officer?"

"Uh-huh, well, finishing up that damage control job you mentioned was the only time I ever failed to obey a direct order."

"How was that?" I asked.

"I put a mattress on a mess table and bolted the whole patch to the main engine room hatch. The skin of the ship had been ruptured, letting seawater come in. We'd already been up two nights by then, and like you say, that water temperature and the lack of sleep sort of put a drain on you. My patch worked great and one "Handy-Billy" [portable pump] could just about keep up with the incoming water, but by now, I'm fagged.

"You may not remember him, but we had a green kid, a Lt. J. G., who had been aboard just a short while. I can't remember

Broached to the beach.

his name, but I'd no more than finished my DC project and leaned back to enjoy it when he came through and examined it.

"'Good job, sailor,' he says. 'But take something and round off them corners.'"

I chuckled and waited. Tex had sort of a hurt look on his face after fifty years. "What did you do?"

"I said, 'I'm sure you can find someone to take off them corners, sir, but I'm going to get a cup of coffee.' I figured they'd throw the book at me, but I never heard a word about it."

I knew Tex had been aboard the LST-1146 when she participated in the Inchon, Korea invasion of September 15, 1950. I went aboard in May of 1952 and had heard the story dozens of times. All centered around the landing being rather routine except that the tremendously high flood tide receded and left the ship high and dry, yards from the waterline.

Some had said they lost power when the sea chest lost contact with the water. Others mentioned being sitting ducks for hours without power for electric gun control. I wanted the straight scuttlebutt. Tex should have it. We'd been shipmates about sixteen months until the war ended.

"Your shooting story have to do with Inchon? If I remember right you were there when the '46 went ashore. I'd like to hear it."

Tex was ready. "We pulled up to that beach and opened our bow doors. The *New Jersey* was shooting over our heads. Boy those sixteen-inch guns made a roar. She was out of sight somewhere behind us. We'd hear the sound of her guns, maybe walk halfway up the deck and light a cigarette, then hear the boom-boom of the shells exploding up there on the beach."

At mention of the battleship *New Jersey*'s sixteen-inch firepower, I thought of Bill Mackey, electrician mate petty officer aboard the USS *Ulvert M. Moore*. In the years I've known Bill, he mentioned a couple of times going ashore to serve as a forward observer in Korea to direct fire for the USS *Missouri*. In a recent phone conversation he'd recalled her being out of sight, but mentioned that the rounds from her big guns were so huge that they were visible coming in over their position.

"I've heard others speak of actually seeing sixteen-inch rounds while they were airborn. You see anything like that?" I asked.

"No, not that I remember, but the vibration of the blast from those shells would actually push the water back from our hull momentarily."

I recalled others talking of overcast conditions at Inchon that day. I also doubted it being classed as a "smoke free zone."

"We had marines with Mark 24 tanks aboard to unload. The North Koreans had Russian Tiger tanks, and the old World War II Shermans our guys were using didn't match up well with them. These new Mark 24s were a welcome sight in Korea in those days. We also had a couple of 6 x 6s on the main deck. You know the deal about the tide there?"

"Story I got was you guys were caught high and dry up on the beach, sort of helpless for quite a while."

"That's partly right. The way I remember, that flood tide was followed with a minor rise and fall then there would be another major tide come in. Anyway we were stuck there for something like 24 hours. But we weren't helpless and we never lost power."

"How? The report I heard was that the sea strainer was on mud, yards from the waterline."

"It was, but yours truly had taken care of that little problem in San Diego weeks before we got to Korea. See we were off the coast of California piddling around with the marines one day, and a school of squid plugged the sea strainer. We cleaned that thing out, and them damn things fouled it again as soon as we turned on the pumps. Well, I got this idea. I rigged an adapter so I could bypass the strainer and go directly to ballast water and circulate it through those engine coolers to keep the auxiliary engines driving those generators. I showed it to the chief and he said, 'Good, make me a bunch of those.' Naw, we didn't lose power; we would have but for that, but we didn't."

★ ★ ★

Corporal Kenneth Wilkinson, with A Co. of the Marine's 1st Engineering Brigade disembarked from another LST at Inchon on the day of the invasion. The ship he rode in also carried a number of M 26 tanks. Wilkinson had seen extensive fighting in the Pusan area before being sent to Inchon for the invasion.

"The resistance we encountered wasn't too great on the beachhead. We came back sometime later and ate there. Some of those LSTs were high and dry. Course, we had to "rib" the swabbies, you know things like, 'What's the matter sailor boy, is your little boat stuck in the mud?'" The ex-marine laughed.

"I had, just a moment before, picked up a Russian-made burp gun some North Korean had lost. A sailor from one of those LSTs walked up and said, 'What will you take for that weapon, marine?'

"'One hundred and fifty dollars,' I said. He didn't bat an eye, just fished in his pocket and handed me the one-fifty. Man, I thought, there's money in war. Well, I stuck that navy money in a pocket and buttoned it down."

★ ★ ★

Like Tex, Bill McGill is and was an excellent diesel mechanic. The three of us were "black-gang" shipmates. They taught me the ropes. I suppose that black-gang name for engine room sailors comes from the period of steam ships and mountains of coal to shovel into boilers, but in our day and with diesel power, it still proved apt.

In speaking of being stranded in Inchon, Bill said. "Tex is right, we were anxious to get off that beach. As soon as that water started lifting us, the old man initiated this rocking motion with the main engines. You saw us try to rock it when they towed us off from being stranded at Coronado. He telegraphed down full astern both engines, then one then the other, but we were stuck fast. He'd stop and maybe you could feel just a slight movement, a little tip this way or that. You know he was a little cautious, maybe timid is better.

"Anyway, I was on the main engines. Me, and I believe it was Antrekan. We tried that rocking stuff a few passes and we ain't budged. Well, the next signal from the bridge came down 'full astern.' We gave the throttles full then reached over to that control rack on the governors for those two main engines and yanked as hard as we could. Talk about wide open, we had it. And we came off!"

★ ★ ★

Tex walked to the coffeepot. He poured himself a cup and tipped the pot in my direction.

I shook off the offer and asked, "So, what about the shooting part?"

Tex sat, "Well, we already mentioned that flood tide. The smart guys, you know the officers that plan all that stuff, had it figured. So many minutes of tide, then we had so many minutes to unload the tanks and get off that beach and back out to sea. Well, it didn't work that way. About the third tank hit one of those raised, cloverleaf chain fasteners. Its track catches and pops a tread. They had to bring up another tank and drag that one off, and by that time we're stuck fast. Now, we got to wait for the next tide.

"My general quarters station is number two loader on the twin 40mm bow guns. I think it was number two; anyway, I handed the clip of rounds to the guy that slammed them into the rack above the breach. We're high on the beach, and I'm looking around. Off a little ways is a railroad track, and I let my gaze follow it over to the left and it disappears around the edge of a mountain that comes down to within yards of the beach.

"The last tank is offloaded, the *New Jersey* has quit firing, and me and everyone else is scanning that beach wondering what is next. Well I hear a noise and see this smoke coming up from behind that rise. There was a steam locomotive back behind there coming toward the bend where the track breaks out into view. We train our guns on that point and wait. It ain't far.

"The word comes from control, 'Fire at will when your target comes into view.' Man, we can't miss! We'll be right on that thing. I envision the rounds exploding in her belly, seeing that boiler blow up. I'm already thinking of painting a freight train on the gun tub. You know, like those hotshot fighter pilots."

I'd never heard this tale before. I remembered Tex as a quiet young man. He's warmed up, enjoying reliving the moment.

"The smoke comes around the bend first then here she comes, passing right in front of us. We cut loose. I see holes appear in her boiler and little puffs of steam, but no explosion. Something's wrong; we got the wrong ordinance or something, I don't know. Maybe we're shooting stuff set to explode at altitude, you know, anti-aircraft. We ought to be blowing that thing into smithereens; instead those rounds just zip right through that little old boiler, and she just finally grinds to a halt not too far from us. She's still setting on that track. Looks like a sieve, but she's not taken an explosive hit. Not one! I never saw human movement of any kind on that train, and that's my shooting war story."

Bill McGill remembered, "I saw a train while we were stranded at Inchon." He said, "I didn't know we shot at it. It sure had a lot of steam coming out of it, though."

Later Tex mentioned a trip to Alaska that he and Maude made. He proudly mentioned achievements at the firehouse in Longview and membership in the Masonic Lodge. It was good to talk to him after all those years. Leaving Longview, I headed the van toward Arkansas and an appointment with Charles W. Hughes.

"Go, Doc, Go!"

The e-mail is dated March 3, 2000. U.S. Navy Corpsman Charles Doc Hughes wrote to an old friend from the Korean War days, Ollen Langston. If I have their relationship correct, in March of 1951 Charles replaced Ollen as 2nd platoon corpsman after "Ollie" had been wounded.

Charles' letter says, "That operation you mentioned when we came under fire riding in those trucks, the way I remember it was we were given orders to go above our own lines to rescue some army paratroop outfit that had been cut off. We were in a truck convoy with two or three tanks leading the way. I think I was in about the fourth truck. When we got to the front line our convoy stopped so the officers could talk to the army unit that held the line there. The army told them we couldn't possibly drive down that road because they had been taking fire from the Chinese, who were directly in front of them.

"After some conferring, our leaders decided orders are orders so our convoy started out again, but we didn't get far. We were in a small valley with the Chinese on the high ground in front and on the ridgelines on either side of the valley, when we came under heavy small arms and mortar fire. A shell landed under the radiator of the first truck, and steam went flying while all of us in the trucks scrambled out and into the ditch. The tank turrets were swinging around trying to find the sources of the incoming to return fire.

"We were relieved to find that there was an unusually deep ditch along the road to give us cover, but you know the lot of the corpsman. I had no more than got hunkered down when the word came down the ditch, 'Doc, they need you up there!'

"At first I thought I might work my way up the ditch, but after one quick try I saw I couldn't get by the marines, so I jumped out on the road and began flying ass toward the front of the column. Mortars were still coming in and there was a deafening roar of small arms fire as I ran along the road. You know, at times like that things are all kind of a blur, but I felt like since I was the only one up on the road and running, all the incoming was aimed at me. Once when I saw a hand waving out of the ditch, I jumped in hoping to have reached the right spot, but the guy had only been pointing me forward. I managed to move a little way up the ditch before I had to jump out on the road again and resume running. The guys were cheering me on, yelling, 'Go, Doc, Go!'

"I finally made it to the first truck and jumped in the ditch and found the wounded guy. I can't remember his name, but I remember what he looked like.

"He was hit in the subclavian artery, and with every beat of his heart blood would spurt out. He was afraid he was bleeding to death, but I told him he would be all right. I put a battle dressing up against the wound and pressed real hard and just held it. I finally grew weary of holding it. My arms were giving out, and I pressed my face against my hands in order to keep the pressure on. My clothes were bloody for days after that, so some of the guys called me "Bloody Doc."

"That marine was evacuated and later recovered okay, as I recall. We called in fire on the ridges around us and were later able to take the ridgeline to our west. And the operation went on, and the action continued, but we never saw that army paratroop outfit."

★ ★ ★

"Those navy corpsmen, they were the best. The medical staff, the doctors we had over in Korea, I can't say they were all that good, but those corpsmen, man!" Corporal Kenneth L. Wilkinson from the Marine's 1st Brigade, A Company, 5th Regiment, spoke with a slight hoarseness to his voice, sort of a rasping sound. In his seventies now, he relived his experiences with me.

"We had some doctors over there that were too quick to amputate limbs from frostbite victims." Wilkinson reminded me of a tough old pro from the fight game. A handsome, mature man, still, faint scars were not entirely hidden. Yes, though he'd look at home in any boxer's corner with a bucket in one hand and a sponge in another, he had earned his fighting skills without benefit of ropes, rules, or bells.

Earlier I learned he received two Purple Hearts, wore a steel plate in his head, and had undergone considerable rearrangement to his nose. He carried other scars. The injuries detailed were related to his second Purple Heart award. He passed off the first as just sort of minor.

Wilkinson said, "We moved out from Inchon, went through the street fighting of Seoul, and were several days north and west of the city the day I got it the last time."

"What were you doing?"

"Walking in front of a tank, looking for mines."

"You were sweeping for mines afoot, in front of a tank?"

The old marine looked at me like one might a cat that had just missed the litter box. You could almost see the mental words "deck ape" form in his eyes. His bottom line contained only one respected navy specialty, and mine had not been that one. Still, we were comfortable together.

He smiled faintly. "I guess you could call it that."

"What happened?"

"I don't know. I became unconscious immediately. Some buddies told me later I took a burst from a burp gun. I woke up on a hospital ship. A navy corpsman did a tracheotomy on me there on the spot."

"Probably saved your life."

"Oh, I'm sure, but you remember that hundred and fifty I told you about, the money I got off of that swab-jockey for that Russian burp gun?"

I nodded.

"I still had it on me when I got hit. One of them danged corpsmen, whoever took my britches off, got away with that money." We both laughed.

"You can't get ahead of the navy," I said.

An hour or so later we finished our interview. Kenneth walked me through his house and then our conversation continued out to the drive where my Dodge was parked. We expressed gratitude to each other and enjoyed another chuckle. I reached for the door handle.

Wilkinson put his hand on my shoulder. "Glad you came by. Take care of yourself. *Semper fi.*"

I paused, looking for something to say. I drew blanks. "Yeah, me too," I stammered. "Anchors a-weigh!" I chuckled.

He grinned and walked halfway back to his front door. I pulled the handle then paused. "What the hell does a sailor say to that?" I asked, laughingly.

Kenneth had a broad grin on his face. He doubled his right fist, extending his thumb and little finger, and turned it up near his mouth like a beer mug. "I said that to a swabby one night in Diego and he did this while saying, 'Yeah, have one for me too.'"

Chapter 21

A Man of Order

Doc Hughes said, "I have often heard men say that if they should be killed, they want it to be quick—instantaneous, without pain or grief. I abhorred such a thought. I wanted to live anyhow, under any circumstances, just as long as I could. My greatest fear was that my consciousness might be taken from me; that I might be hit in the head; that I might be hurled into the abyss in a split second. I often pondered such an end. I even had recurring dreams about it in which I perceived what it might be like—a small bright orange starburst in my skull, then..."

Charlie's notes continued, "Today, as I ran behind Hutchins, I muttered my old totally selfish and frantically sincere prayer, 'Don't let me die. God! Don't let me die! Please, God, don't let me die!'

"Earlier that morning when I got back to camp, I found that Smitty had worked on our tent. He had apparently taken a branch or piece of brush and swept the ground all around, for the area was completely smooth and free of pebbles and twigs. He had also gathered a bunch of white chalk rocks and outlined a walk in front of the tent shaped like a cross. Everything was neat. It had to be so with Smitty, for he carried his order about him, wore it like a cloak. He superimposed it on the most random and chaotic circumstances. When you share shelter halves with a person, you appreciate such things.

"We made the line of trees and found a dry creek bed. The lieutenant screamed into the hand radio, trying to be heard over the artillery that had begun to thunder again.

"Smitty was about five yards to my right. I turned to say something to him but stopped. He lay on his back looking up into the trees. He had that agitated look in his eyes, perhaps disturbed by the disorder, still, he grinned."

Charlie Hughes described the struggle for "The Crag." It was the day he saved Sergeant Hardie Richards' life. A lot of other things happened that day. After describing Richards' wound and the treatment he administered to him, Charlie continued with a description of the day's activity at the Crag.

"The battle, which had raged for some hours now, was being fought for the strip of high ground that lay in front of the trenches. The North Koreans held a position similar to ours at the other end of the strip. They made six or seven attempts to dislodge the marines from the trenches. They paid severely for each attempt. Now something in the sounds of battle, perhaps a lessening of fire from the enemy trenches, signified the moment.

"I jerked my head up to the sound of yelling and saw marines pouring from the trenches and disappearing over the rise. I finished tying a battle dressing on a man's leg and started up the slope. I cleared a trench with a leap and found myself running behind a clutter of screaming marines. I had not taken ten steps when it hit. There was a black flash above us. My head and chest were crushed with pressure, and instantly I thought of death.

"When I came to my senses, I found myself on my hands and knees looking back at the spot where I'd been running. My eyes burned, my head ached, and my mouth and nose were filled with the acrid sting of gunpowder. I examined myself quickly and found everything intact.

"They have us zeroed in, flashed through my mind. Gripped with panic, I jumped to my feet and started to run back to the trenches. Then I heard them. Their voices came from several directions."

We were in Charlie's study at his house in Arkansas. "I didn't write it that way," he said, "but I know now what hit us was one of our own 'short' rounds. Had it been enemy fire zeroed in that well, it would have been over for all of us."

His notes continued. "'Corpsman! Corpsman! Help me, Doc.... Oh, please, God, help me...SOMEBODY HELP ME!'

"I turned, cringing, and started back across the strip. I saw something gray and colorless lying on the ground like a large misshapen stone. I leaned over it and could see that it was a guy I knew. He lay face up. Both his legs were blown off just below the groin. One of his arms was missing except for the hand and a long ribbon of flesh, which held it to his shoulder. Strangely, there was little blood.

"I bent to his powder-blackened face. 'Hey Guy!' Two great, bright blue eyes shot open. Good God, he's alive, I thought. I felt helpless and sick.

"'Do you hurt bad?' I heard myself ask.

"'No, not bad.' The blasted man was strangely lucid. He turned his head slightly and with his good arm reached across his body and retrieved the other hand. The livid string of flesh dangled crazily as he laid the detached hand carefully on his chest. He closed his eyes.

"I scratched desperately through my bag for dressings large enough to cover the stumps of his legs. There were none. I hated him. Terrible thoughts raced through my head. There was nothing I could do. Why don't you die? You ought to be dead! Why don't you die? Another corpsman arrived and we did get this fatally wounded man bandaged.

"I jumped up and started moving again. The sounds of fighting had swept forward on the mountain and were beginning to subside. I heard someone calling faintly just down the eastern slope. As I neared I saw a green helmet poking out of a shallow shell hole. I dropped into the hole and found myself face to face with Smitty. He was sitting up holding his knee and rocking gently back and forth. The kneecap was gone and jagged white bones protruded from the gray flesh.

"'Smitty?'"

Charlie took his notes from me. His face was calm, serious. "Mackey, when I wrote about this I used fictitious names, tried to fictionalize the story. It's really all true. The guy I called Grover in these notes is really Smitty. I didn't know Richard's name at the time."

Charlie took a pen and wrote in the actual names. He wrote Smitty where he'd had Grover. We agreed to leave the guy who'd lost the limbs unnamed. I sensed a struggle within this new friend. His eyes opened slightly wider and I turned away to hide my own emotion. God, how quickly I felt connected to this man.

Charlie continued the story, "Smitty?"

"'I'm hurt, Doc.' There was terror in his voice.

"'You'll be okay,' I said, binding his knee with a battle dressing.

"'My back too, I think I'm hit back there.'

"'Let's take a look.' I cut his shirt away and found a shallow three-inch gash high up on his back. 'You got a flesh wound here, but you'll be all right.' I bandaged the wound as well as I could, talking all the while.

"'I still feel it, on farther down.' His voice sounded strained and shrill. I tore his shirt on down and exposed a huge gaping hole at his waist. Blood and water oozed from the wound. Without realizing it, I suddenly stopped talking.

"'What is it, Doc?' Smitty pleaded.

"'You got another place down here, but it's not bad. You'll be all right,' I lied.

"'Am I going to be all right?'

"'Sure, sure. All you got is a good ticket back to Japan, maybe even the States.'

"Smitty's skin turned the color of ashes, his breathing more shallow and dry. I fixed the wound as well as I could, removed his helmet, and leaned him back against the side of the hole and looked into his face. His features were frozen into an expression of inarticulate horror. He viewed his torn and unresponsive body with disbelief. The simple design that he inherited and nurtured had begun to crumble weeks ago. Now, his mortal wounds were the final debacle. Death moved swiftly, inexorably to engulf him—and he did not know why. I imagined he believed death must have a reason as did life, an order.

"'Am I going to die?' he looked imploringly into my face.

"'No, you're not going to die, Smitty. You got a ticket out of here that's all.' I tried to say it convincingly, but I could see he didn't believe me. I could see the terror he was trying to shut from his mind. His wild eyes sought something . . . something!

"I dug his Bible from his pack and put it in his hands. He held it disconsolately to his breast. He visibly weakened and began to grimace with pain. I gave him a shot of morphine then leaned back against the side of the hole across from him. Slowly his features relaxed from the morphine and from the redeeming indifference of approaching death.

"All that remained of the battle were a few popping rifle reports coming from somewhere down the northern slope. Marines moved back and forth on the strip at a more casual pace. Across from me in the hole, Smitty's face had turned to wax. He leaned back against the beveled wall, his head tilted slightly toward his right shoulder. The lips that modestly covered the large front teeth during life relaxed. His eyes were almost closed.

"In death Smitty looked like a little boy, a child. And now, years later as a parent myself, I realize that he was a child and that we were all children, really. Wars are always fought by someone's children.

"The battle was over. The little strip of ground that we had fought so long for, devastated. It looked like the surface of the moon, barren and pockmarked. Nothing remained but blasted trees and brittle dust.

"Men gathered in clusters and began to recount events of the battle. Some marines built fires and began to heat food for it was now after noon. I borrowed a fire and warmed a can of beans. As I ate the beans, I thought of Smitty; I thought of his parents and my own dubious future.

"I would rig my shelter half by itself from now on. I could do it. I had seen it done. It would not be as snug, but it would work, and I preferred it that way. But somehow I knew it would lack Smitty's touch."

Chapter

22

Trackless Skies and
Quiet Depths

$\mathbf{C}$ontrol of airspace like that of the ground in Korea was fickle and bought at a horrific price. Doc Hughes mentioned looking down into a picturesque view of a valley one evening. He attempted to put closure on an ugly day of fighting. I believe the date was May 31, 1951. Shadows were deepening and before him on the valley floor nestled a battalion aid station.

The distance diminished the scattered tents' appearance into doll-like structures. There was little to suggest the valiant work underway there except the choppers, jeeps, and ambulances arriving at intervals with precious cargoes.

Beyond the corpsman in the opposite direction was a higher range of rugged mountains that belonged to the enemy. Charles said, "As I watched, the sounds of propellers came to me and I turned to see three F-4 U Corsairs. They flew almost in wingtip contact with each other and barely cleared the last enemy ridgeline. A trail of smoke or vapor came from the middle plane. Seconds later they were over my valley, and each wingman broke formation in opposite direction. The aircraft in the center flipped over on its back directly above the aid station. With the canopy back, the pilot dropped from his plane. A moment later his chute opened and he drifted down to the waiting arms of the medical staff below."

All pilots were not so lucky as the one the corpsman watched that evening. The other side had a good plane in the MiG-15. It was so good our side went to great lengths attempting to get our hands on one. There were things about them our intelligence people would like to know. The plan was to reverse engineer the craft a piece at a time to gain insight into the characteristics that gave it superior acceleration to our aircraft. March and McElfresh detail at length some of the efforts our side expended to obtain that information in a chapter referred to as "Pinch-A-Mig" in their book previously referred to.

At the same time, the Soviet Union's mouth watered in anticipation of learning more about the USAF F-86 Fs being used successfully against their fighters near the Yalu River. Not only did they want a plane, but they also wanted a pilot of the downed craft. This was the setting Captain Troy G. Cope and his wingman flew into on 16 September 1952. Captain Cope never returned from that mission. Some think he may have ultimately ended up in the Soviet Union.

Captain Cope's brother, Carl Cope of Ennis Texas, handed me a report turned in by his brother's wingman. It described the day's events as follows. "Captain Cope and I were briefed to fly a two-ship formation of Jato equipped F-86 Fs on a fighter sweep along the Yalu River. This was near Lake Sui-ho. Prior to takeoff, we agreed to fly a floating lead, that is, whoever possessed the better advantage would assume the lead, with the other flying his wing.

Captain Troy Gordon Cope (MIA)

"Shortly after crossing the Chongchon-gang we spotted two flights of four MiGs headed north. As Capt. Cope was officially leader, he followed the flight he had in sight until about 20-25 miles south of Lake Sui-ho two more MiGs crossed in front of us. Captain Cope broke off his attack on the first four, which were pretty far away, and made an attack on these MiGs. They broke and we made a 360 and came out headed north at about 36,000 feet with Capt. Cope 2,000 feet behind the trailing MiG and myself 1,500 feet or so behind Captain Cope and about 1,000 feet to his left. Captain Cope fired his Jato and then commenced firing on this MiG. He pulled away slightly from me, but the pair of MiGs pulled away from both of us. I observed no hits on this MiG, but was in a poor position for accurate observation.

"My airplane was slightly faster than Captain Cope's and after he ran out of ammo, I was almost line abreast with him. At that time we observed some more MiGs coming up on us from the rear. I asked Captain Cope to call the break, and he replied, 'Roger, take it left, now.'

"After completing a 180, I looked back and saw three MiGs behind me, Cope and three more MiGs behind him. After two complete turns the MiGs gave up and we rejoined. At that time Captain Cope informed me he was out of ammo, and for me to take over the lead. We were then at 30,000 feet. I took up a course paralleling the Yalu about 10 miles south of the border and headed downstream towards Antung. We made two bounces, once on F-86s, once on MiGs, which beat us to the border. We headed south after that bounce and ran into two MiGs headed towards the river about 10 miles due south of the city of Antung. I made a turn to the right and was falling slightly in trail of those MiGs when I spotted three more MiGs following them. I flattened my turn and called these MiGs out to Cope. As I was approaching a line abreast position with these MiGs I saw three more behind these. I called Cope and asked him if he had 'those other three MiGs.' He acknowledged this transmission. I'm not certain if he knew which three I was referring to. But at that time I was too far committed to break off without becoming a target for the first three."

Carl Cope speaks fondly of his brother's wingman who came home alone. Doc Hughes found the hills of Korea to be, at times, a lonely place for corpsmen. For some, the skies were no friendlier. The surviving airman is Karl E. Dittmer, Captain USAF.

Captain Troy Gordon Cope has not been heard from since that fateful flight. As mentioned in his biography, his dog tags have shown up in a Chinese Korean War museum. An American businessman brought pencil rubbings of the tags back to this country. The long vigil continues.

★ ★ ★

Ed Buckman, a carrier sailor, mentioned the loss of fliers. "My job on the *Princeton* included checking out the pilot as soon as he landed to find out if all his electronic equipment worked well. On December 24, 1950, I worked on Ensign H. V. Scarsheim's helmet. He had broken a wire on it during an air strike the day before. I soldered on the helmet when my chief petty officer walked by. He noticed what I was doing and recognized the headgear.

"'You can put that away,' he said, 'We lost Scar today.'

"I finished it anyway, but I lost a friend that day."

Ed paused a moment; he glanced at the weeks old great-grandbaby he baby-sat while we talked. "The flight deck of a carrier is a dangerous place. One day we had all but one plane down safely. This plane had a 265-pound frag bomb snagged beneath it. The pilot tried unsuccessfully to release it at sea and was getting dangerously low on fuel.

"Well, they gave him the okay to make an approach, but at the last moment waved him off. He gunned the engine. That jarred the bomb loose. I was standing at midship and it looked like the thing was coming down my throat. I dived for a hatch and down I went. Luckily for me, I was third to reach it or I would have broken both arms. The sailors before me broke my fall.

"The bomb's propeller did not have enough rotations to arm it, and it stuck nose-first in the wooden deck. Two brave ordinance men removed it and dropped it overboard."

A little before my chat with Buckman, I caught up with Carl Kisinger by phone late one evening in September 2001. We'd visited at my father's funeral a couple of months earlier. I could hear tiredness in Carl's voice, but contentment also registered there. He'd spent the day mowing on his farm and capped the evening off at twilight watching deer come out of the brakes to feast on the newly mown coastal grass. Our conversation drifted back to the days of Korea.

Carl's three-and-half-year naval career was spent aboard aircraft carriers, flattops. He received his discharge as a 3rd Class PO Aviation Electronic Technician. The evening we talked Carl stumbled a little naming his old ships. "There was the *Essex*, the *Antietam*, and the *Yorktown*," he said. "The *Essex* is the one I spent most of my time on in Korean waters."

"You guys lost some men and planes out there," I prompted.

"We did. It was before steam catapults; we were using hydraulics in those days. We didn't have the twelve-foot barriers then, either. Yeah, we lost a number of pilots and several men from the deck crew."

We didn't dwell on the events. I had heard them before, watched Carl, as a young man, stare into a beer and try to make sense of it. Death reduced to a routine makes no sense. I thought of the ocean view from the fantail of my ship, the screw's turbulence fading within the dim wake, a faint path rising on swell after swell, dipping into the troughs then ultimately disappearing in the distance.

Brave men who joined those distant swells live today in the memories of their loved ones, yet they are increasingly lost to dim memories of some who served with them and knew them only casually. Suddenly, I too sensed a waning of energy at day's end. Still, it was good to pick up a phone and talk to someone you'd shared the fire of youth with.

"Remember the night I came aboard the *Essex* when you were tied up at Oakland and my ship was over at Treasure Island. It made an impression on me. I'd never seen so much steel in my life. And it floated," I laughed. "We went into Frisco that night."

"I don't remember," Carl said.

I chuckled to myself. That was one moment of failed memory that might not be totally caused by age on either of our parts. One of us helped the other to bed that night. It was the blind leading the blind. Like Carl, I'm unsure who did the steering.

I thought of Doc Hughes watching three gull-winged Corsairs bring an injured airman home. The question of Captain Cope's fate, the years he'd missed watching his boys grow, gnawed at my contentment. Some of my own impatience at war's disorder returned. I remembered a mangled-legged, baby-faced vet's reply in a 1951 hospital ward to a friend's question. He had recently returned from his physical review-board session.

"So what do you think, Pard? What you gonna do for a living out there?" the friend asked.

The young man, too quickly grown old, shrugged while violently grinding out his cigarette. "I dunno. I hear they's good money in whorehouses."

It's difficult to wave the flag incessantly. It's heavier some days than others.

Chapter 23

Friendly Beaches— Dangerous Liberty

"**W**e arrived at the Port of Pusan on August 3, 1950. The Marine Band greeted us. We went over on the USS *Henrico*, I believe it was. We'd been cooped up on that thing for a long time and were ready to hit the beach, any kind of beach." Kenneth Wilkinson talked and I took notes, sitting on his patio in Carrolton, Texas.

He said. "We'd left Camp Pendleton around July 15. You look at so much water you're ready for a change of scenery. That band pumped our blood. And they were playing for us.

"Well, they had a chain strung along there, some ways in front of that band, and we all crowded up to it. There was a sea-going, deck ape of a jar head; you know, a marine guard assigned to the fleet, and he came down that chain hollering, 'Stand clear, stand back, six feet behind the line, marines.' He banged his club against that chain, not giving a damn how many fingers and knuckles he busted. Guys were hollering, shaking their fingers, cussing.

"I stepped back before he got to me. I looked the other way a moment then heard more cussing then a loud splash. When I turned, there that guard was floundering around in the drink. He busted one knuckle too many, and the guy grabbed him and threw him in. He was pissed.

"We received bandoleers of live ammunition and disembarked shortly afterwards. It was our last music for a while. At least we were off that ship."

★ ★ ★

Most Korean veterans have a train story. Tex Owens remembered shooting holes in one at Inchon. Others told of having them stop while they fell out to take cover from various types of fire. Some mentioned the unbelievable amount of people and cargo that were packed aboard. Glen Thompson was sent to Korea to man a machine gun. Later he discovered the rail service of the South Koreans held hazards of its own. He mentioned a little narrow-gauge Korean "choo-choo" that said it could, but couldn't.

"We loaded on this thing while it sat puffing and were soon underway. I wasn't sure it would ever roll, but it did. Looking back today, I think of the little children's train story, the one that says, 'I can, I can.'

"On a steep grade, the train strained and groaned; the rails squeaked and screeched; everyone leaned forward as if to help the train up the mountain. It slowed and someone said, 'Hey, the train is stopped.'

"'No,' someone said, 'it's moving backward.'

"'Someone stop this train!'

"The locomotive gained speed. Scenery, which had crept by on the way up, flashed by on the way down. The train rocked.

"'Where's the brakeman?'

"'Lord, I hope there's not a train behind us.'

"Eventually, the thing shot out onto the plain below and rolled to a stop. The engineer put it in reverse and backed it a few miles where he delayed several minutes. One could imagine a fireman shoveling coal like crazy, watching that pressure climb.

"We started slowly but gathered speed until we reached the base of the mountain at full speed. Although the train slowed considerably on the steep grade, this time it climbed the mountain."

★ ★ ★

War offered a lot of risk. Even travel and off-duty times were filled with peril.

Liberty, a night on the beach, overnight passes, all summon visions of happiness. But most noncommissioned military personnel's off-duty time is spent traveling through or wallowing in a skid row environment. This is particularly true of the unmarried. Generalizations are dangerous, and there are always exceptions. Unfortunately, in this case there are few. Most are too young to legally purchase alcohol. They are forced to seek the shadowy dives to desperately boost a self-image of toughness. If the military doesn't make the young recruit angry enough and give him reason to fight, the surroundings on liberty will provide it.

Stepping off the boat, through the gate, or from the taxi, the young seaman, soldier, airman, or marine steps boldly, often admirably valiant, even touchingly kind, into the stench of the forgotten waterfront or the cantankerous traffic. In the words of Robert Louis Stevenson, "We find in him the thought of duty, the thought of something owing to himself, to his neighbor, to his God." He carries with him, "An ideal of decency, to which he would rise if it were possible; a limit of shame below which, if it be possible, he will not stoop."

Still in his simple youth, "The vile pleasures of the fiddle in a tavern, a bedizened trull who sells herself to rob him" are more temptation than most withstand. Truly the discard of society, the fool, the thief, and the comrade of thieves repay his service with scorn. His fists clench, his teeth grit, and he lashes out at friend and foe alike. Shipmates draw steel prepared to cut their way through their closest friend for the last can of beer or a half-smoked butt. Somewhere in this night a door will be passed, a door through which there is no return.

After a few months on the front line, it's a safe bet Glen Thompson would have found little in the toughest of the world's slums to worry about. He had some time to serve in Korea after the armistice. He told the following story:

"We had a guy in our outfit named Cy. The war was over, time hung heavy, and Cy went AWOL. He found some hootch somewhere, and he came back loaded. He was a good soldier, well liked, and we'd all been through a lot together, but something had to be done.

"We had a sergeant, a twenty-year man, gray headed, tough, and not too far from retirement. He pointed at Cy's M-1 and said, 'Give me your weapon.'

"The soldier stared a minute, grinned at the sergeant, and handed over the rifle. 'Give me your bayonet,' the sergeant said.

"Cy shook his head.

"The sergeant pulled his .45 and said, 'Your bayonet, Cy, give it to me.'

"'No,' he replied.

"The sergeant palmed back the receiver of the .45, pointed it at Cy's stomach, and said, 'This is your last chance, give me the bayonet.'

"Cy cussed the noncom and said, 'No.'

"The sergeant pulled the trigger, the gun clicked, and I liked to have dropped in my tracks. I had a vision of guts blasted all over that mountain."

"It didn't fire?" I asked.

"No, it didn't fire and then he ejected and snapped each round in turn until the clip emptied. He went in the tent and got another clip and did the same thing with each round in it. Each time he'd ask Cy for the bayonet and Cy would refuse and cuss the sergeant. I guess he was too drunk to fight or run. I don't know what he had found to drink, but whatever it was had a kick.

"Finally the sergeant looked at those of us standing there and said, 'Men, get that man's bayonet.'

"We wrestled him to the ground and that was that, but I sure thought Cy was a dead man that day.

"The sergeant stalked down to supply with that pistol in his hand and threw it on the clerk's table. 'What's wrong with this damn .45?'

"The clerk examined it and pointed at a broken firing pin. 'You carry this on the line?' He asked. The sergeant had already turned and was walking away."

★ ★ ★

Thompson paused and leaned back in his chair. He stared at the ceiling. A moment later he lowered his gaze.

"We had a KATUSA with us for a while."

"A what?" I asked.

"It stands for Korean Auxiliary temporarily assigned to the U.S. Army, something like that. He was an ROK soldier but assigned to our company. He was a good man, fought well. He was mostly used as an ammo bearer, but we all got along well with him. He would ultimately go back to a Korean unit. I don't know how you spell his name, but he pronounced it something like the Arkansas hog call, 'Sue-ee.'

"Well, after the armistice this guy got in a scrape of some kind. I guess it was with some Korean buddies. I never did know the details, but it was some minor transgression. That was all it took though. Once he was written up, it was automatically back to the Koreans for him and maybe a few years in prison. They were rough on stuff like that.

"My buddy Burns and I got selected to escort Sue-ee back to Katusa prison south of Seoul. We arrived in Seoul late one evening and decided to spend the night there; then in the morning we would take our prisoner on down to Katusa. He'd tried his best to talk us into going by his nearby village so he could see his family. He knew he was out of circulation for a long time, if not forever. We wanted to oblige, as we liked the guy, but we knew better. We checked him in with the MPs in Seoul for the night and hit the streets.

"It was our first time in Seoul, and the town teemed with military. They were all polished, bloused trousers, creased caps, and jackets. It was spit-and-polish, show time. You can imagine our appearance. We were a week away from our one bath in forty days, scuffed boots and combat jackets that defied description. We still had on steel pots.

"We hadn't gone fifty feet when two MPs grabbed us. 'Hey, soldiers you're out of uniform. You damn guys are a disgrace to the U.S. Army,' they growled. It was back to MP headquarters and boot polish and borrowed caps and jackets before they let us out on our own."

★ ★ ★

A steel pot was uniform of the day when Kenneth Wilkinson fought through Seoul earlier in the war. The helmet would cover a little thinner hair today. Still, he looks fit. From all appearances, he might have easily been the one to dispatch the overbearing, knuckle-busting guard he told of earlier. He proudly mentioned Native American heritage and responded,

"Sioux," when I asked what tribe. When his heritage was brought to my attention, I noticed faint but classic features, the dark eyes and handsome profile that I so longed for as a boy and that supported his claim. He mentioned a term I'd not heard in ages.

"When we were in Pendleton a group of marines went to L.A. on liberty. They encountered a gang of "zoot-suiters" and something happened. It ended with two marines stabbed. I believe one may have died. Anyway we loaded a couple of train cars and went up and cleaned that place out."

Wilkinson and trouble are no strangers. One seems to pursue the other. After his second Purple Heart injury, he found himself on the USS *Consolation*. Near death after stopping a North Korean burp gun's blast, he was somehow routed with army patients instead of marines. He ended up in Tokyo General Hospital trying to convince the staff he was marine not army. He was later forwarded on to Yokosuka, with a plate in his head, a healing broken clavicle, and a nose that has been disarranged. He was later sent to Bethesda Naval Hospital for plastic surgery.

Wilkinson took me back to those days in Maryland. "There was a ward nurse at Bethesda, a Lieutenant Neely. I called her Captain. I don't think she liked that. Well, they were having a dance there on the base for navy only. Course I was marine. I'm bitching about being stuck in that damn place and this sailor, a corpsman about my size, says, 'I'll bring my dress whites over and see if you can't wear them. If you can, crash that damn dance.'

"The whites fit. He shows me how to block that white hat like they wore them in those days then gets called away. I'm looking in the mirror fingering that neckerchief. Well, I wrap her under that stupid flap and fumble around a bit with that knot. After awhile I just say, 'to hell with it.' I can't get it right.

I'm a little testy in those days. To make a long story short, I give up and slap a good-looking Windsor knot in that thing.

"I get to that dance and everybody in the place is looking at me. This sailor comes over and motions me to follow him. He leads me into the head and changes that Windsor to a square knot and I'm ready to roll.

"Back on the dance floor somebody taps me on the shoulder and I turn. It's Lt. Neely.

"'May I have this dance?' she asks, feigning sweetness.

"'Sure,' I say, thinking my good looks are saving my life.

"We make a couple of moves and she tilts her head and looks me in the eye. 'Wilkinson, I hope you like buffing floors, 'cause your ass is tied to that cleaning detail for as long as you are in my ward.'

"She wasn't teasing."

Beyond the Front

"'Take the Little Indian with you.' That's me they are talking about," Wilkinson said. "I'm the Little Indian, part Sioux, but this is Korea. They think I can see in the dark. I hate patrol. We were supposed to have tank support on our left flank, and the captain wanted to know how far they extended.

"So we went, quiet, barely moving, scared to death. We stumbled around, I don't know, every communist in Asia must have known we were out there. I couldn't see nothing. After what seemed like hours of this, we sort of felt our way along a ditch or ravine or something, a depression of some kind. Well I'm on the point, of course. I creep up this incline and stick my head through these bushes. I'm looking straight into the muzzle of the biggest cannon I ever saw.

"At first, I don't know if it's ours or theirs, but then we hear whispered English and my heart revives. Of course the gun's mounted on one of our tanks, and we've accomplished our mission, but one little Indian has just about wet his pants. I think,

I've had it. Normally those muzzles point above your head. They had that thing pointed down and across that depression."

Corporal Marvin Dunn, of 1-1-1 Able Co. arrived in Pusan, Korea on August 1, 1951. The corporal's weapon was a BAR. "It will fire 360 rounds a minute with the proper ammunition feed. Sometimes you need all of it. Still, even though it's fully automatic, you train yourself that there are times you squeeze off only one shot at a time. Automatic fire draws a lot of attention."

On September 10 Able Company moved up Hill 749 to replace the 7th. At midnight Marvin pulled the first watch. "My buddy, an ammo carrier, shared my hole. He tried to grab a few winks while I maintained a lookout. Before us was a valley, maybe 300 yards in width. You could see it in the light of mortar flares. They would fire one about every three minutes. It would light things up for maybe forty-five seconds.

"All of a sudden North Koreans filled the valley, swarming like a mass of ants. They were throwing grenades, firing, blowing whistles, banging bells, and screaming. It was deafening. At daylight you could look across there and the place was covered with bodies.

"There are things you try to forget about war. I don't believe many talk about them. I don't know. I've never mentioned it, but the odor... powder, cordite, smoke, burnt flesh, and the smoldering fires," Dunn paused. A moment later he continued.

"The next day at 10 A.M. we were ordered to take another hill. Our company commander, a 2nd lieutenant, took the point. A burp gun caught him right between the eyes. It was 2 P.M. when we secured that hill. Two days later we dug in on Hill 884. We were there about thirty days. Then we went back into reserve on the skyline of another hill.

"We had a command post bunker there along that ridge. That's where I got it. God was trying to tell me something that day. The official version according to the marines is that I stepped on a mine. I'd almost swear it was incoming. Whatever, the results were the same. I lost my lower leg and foot. I was carrying logs in my arms to reinforce the bunker. Otherwise the shrapnel would have killed me. The guys said those logs were riddled."

★ ★ ★

PFC Glen Thompson arrived in Inchon in the spring of 1953. A short time later, traveling in deuce-and-a-half trucks, they watched the distant and dark horizon light occasionally with flashes and listened to the dull "boom-boom-boom" of artillery. "I don't know if it was the shells exploding or the guns firing," Glen said.

"Pockets of light danced on the horizon, creating jagged, semicircular displays of artillery fire. The night was about us. Heavy muzzle flashes lit up our right front. At each replacement depot—we stopped at three that night—we heard the same story. 'The Chinese soldier is the best night fighter in the world. He will spend all night creeping ten feet toward you.'

"I remember coming into the 2nd Battalion Headquarters and one of the COs interviewed us. He was a good man, a lieutenant colonel, I believe. 'I want you men to know,' he said, 'I won't leave you. Whatever happens, if you get cut off out there anywhere, we're coming after you. I'll send a platoon. If they can't get you, we'll send a company; if that doesn't work, I'll send the whole damn battalion. And remember, the Chinese soldier is a good night fighter.'

"Before long, we are out of the truck, marching single file on either side of the road, yards apart in proper military manner. We had chow at noon and it's dark now. The 155s are going over us. One guy says, 'We're going to the front.'

"'Can't be,' I say. 'It's too quiet.'

"Soon we're in these trenches with a good view of nothing but darkness across the valley. The sergeant some of us report to jerks a thumb toward some nearby trenches. 'Turks,' he says, 'Don't talk to the Turks. Don't, for God's sake, get them agitated.'

"Of course, we're bug-eyed by now, Chinese in front, Turks to our flank. We later learned the Turks are tough and damn good fighters. They nearly all carried these curved looking knives. I did see a couple of 'em agitated once. They snarled, 'Turks, punch'ee—punch'ee Chinks.' I nodded agreement.

"It's pitch dark and we all know there is no one beyond us but the enemy. The sergeant takes me over to a more dense blackness, a hole in the ground. It's just the two of us. 'That's your position,' he says under his voice. It's a cave, covered at the top. It wasn't built by our guys, of that I'm sure.

"I felt my way down in the dark. It's deep and near the bottom is an opening into the light of the outside night. I see the silhouette of a machine gun and by touch, determine its one of ours, a .30-caliber, water cooled. It's loaded, ready to go. I'm fixed up but alone—no ammo assistant—just me, the dark, and this weapon I know so well.

"Outside now, parachute flares light up the area in front of me. Barbed wire entanglements extend along and down the slope for fifteen or twenty yards. Down the line sporadic rifle fire snaps through the night, and in the distance a machine gun raps. Moments later flares drift down their wobbly path, and everything in the bare landscape appears to have movement. I squint. There's nothing there. Is that a prone figure, the landscape, or a Chinese inching along? I squint again. The flares go out. It's dark.

"Behind me a distant but strong voice says, 'hold your fire.'

"The tarnished light of a flare brightens the scene again, and I find the same prone figure. It's not too far out, well in range. I think I saw it move. If I fire, I give away this machine gun position. Did I really see it move? The flares go out again. I wait.

"More light. I pull my .45, hold it, then reholster it. I remember the firing range and my chances of hitting anything beyond arm's length with that thing. I pick up the figure over the machine gun's sights. I believe it is moving. I rip off a couple of bursts of fire and see the figure shudder. The light fades again.

"Someone hollers, 'Hold your fire. Who fired those rounds?' I don't make a peep. All night I keep quiet, sweating blood. The next morning in the dim first light I make out the bullet riddled form of a log where my prone figure of the night before had been."

Chapter 25

The First Shot

Larry Zellers likely heard some of the first firing that took place in the Korean War. He lived at Kaesong on the morning of June 25, 1950. Accustomed to such intermittent fire after a couple of years in that area, he paid little attention. In the country as a civilian missionary and teacher, action on his part was not expected. He tried to return to sleep.

Some give little thought to firing at the enemy. Others choose to serve in other capacities. A few, perhaps hiding behind bravado, pretend to relish the thought of firing at others. Those of us never exposed to the necessity of squeezing off a round at another human have little idea of our own reaction.

Navy Corpsman Charles Hughes handed me his written account of the following event when we visited in his home. His earlier paragraphs had set the scene. The action took place in the winter of 1950-51 near Pohang. Assigned to the 1st platoon of Howe Co. 3rd Battalion, 7th Regiment, 1st Marine Division, Doc Hughes referred to the mission as "a guerrilla hunt."

"Lt. Lowe yelled out, 'Get the son-of-a-bitch!'

"I had been holding the man in the sights of my carbine braced against a tree. Although it would fire full automatic, I had it set on semiautomatic. As soon as I heard the lieutenant's words, I squeezed off three rapid shots and saw three white spots appear on the ice right behind the running man. Then a marine near me let go with his BAR. The black-figured guerrilla hit the ice and slid to a stop and did not move.

"After the shooting started someone yelled out, 'There they go!'

"Six or seven guerrillas ran through a ravine behind the village. The light machine guns, BARs, and M-1s opened up, but the North Koreans disappeared down the ravine. All the fire then turned to the houses. Marines fired small .61 mortars, but the village was so steeply below us that the mortars pointed almost straight up and the shells seemed to take forever to land. When they did, puffs of white phosphorus showed they were way off target. The machine guns and BARs were deadly effective. I could see tracers crisscrossing and lacing through the mud walls and grass roofs of the houses.

"Shortly after we opened fire, an old man and small girl perhaps eight years old emerged from one of the houses. They stood by the door facing us, the old man with his hand on the girl's shoulder, both looking up toward us, toward the trees that were our cover. They stood there for just a few seconds then went back in the house.

"By the time the mortars found the target, the village was already on fire from the tracers. Smoke rose from every thatched roof. I had been watching to see if the old man or little girl would appear again, but they never did. The house burned fiercely. I don't know how many were in the village, but the only ones we saw escape were the guerrillas who fled down the ravine.

"When there seemed no point in trying to inflict further damage, Lt. Lowe gave the order to cease fire. We sat there for a while watching the village burn. The houses blazed and blackened, and smoke and embers and whiffs of black straw, the only component of the village to escape, blew away in the wind, blew down the valley, away from our position.

"Most of us were fresh replacements at the time, but two of the veterans of the Chosin Reservoir were talking:

"'We took a hill just outside Yudam-ni. We came up on the ridgeline and there was this wounded Chinese captain sitting up against a tree in the snow just looking at us. He wore something red on his chest like a ribbon or medal, and old Arnold there bet me he could hit it with his M-1 from where we stood, so I took the bet, a case of beer when we get back to the States.'

"'Did he hit it?'

"'Hell no!' Arnold spoke up. 'I missed it by two inches, but I got something out of it. It wasn't a ribbon anyway; it was a God-damn fountain pen. I sold it to one of them rear echelon pogues back there in Masan.'

"All the way down the mountain, throughout the rest of the day and that night in my sleeping bag, I kept seeing the figure of the man running along the ice, the white spots exploding behind him and his body sliding face down along the frozen river. I thought about the old man and the little girl. They must be dead; no one in that village could have escaped. There must have been other civilians in there we never saw.

"I surprised myself being the first one to fire at the man on the ice. I wasn't the one who killed him, but that was just a technicality. I had tried. Since World War II navy corpsmen and army medics were issued carbines for their own protection, but they were not required to use them. The old noncombatant approach with the red crosses on the helmets had not worked. The crosses just made good targets.

"We replacements felt some awe and a little envy when it came to the veterans of the Chosin campaign, but I couldn't think much of Arnold and his friend. What do cold-blooded bastards like that do when they go back to civilian life? Do they make good husbands and fathers and friends? Or are some guys just psychopaths who control their impulses until war gives them license.

"With few exceptions, we weren't psychopaths. Still, look at what happened that other day when the black dog ran into the field of fire. And today, why was I the first to shoot? Why did I even shoot? I would wonder about that over the coming days and weeks, and I would continue to see that body slide down the ice.

"I found out while we were on that patrol that there was a name on the lieutenant's map for the village we destroyed. It was Kitty Dong."

★ ★ ★

Charles Smith said, "My unit originally known as the California's 40th Division of the National Guard was called early into Korea. They were not well trained, well equipped, or well

40th Division on the move
Photo courtesy of Charles Smith

Winter, another enemy for the 224th Regiment 40th Division. Charles Smith's Heavy Mortar Co. *Photo courtesy of Charles Smith*

led. They performed no better in the face of overwhelming odds. Governor Warren recalled the entire division, and the military set about to correct the situation. I was among the replacements. After arriving in Pusan, Korea, during May or June of 1952, I was assigned to Company M (Heavy Weapons), 224 Regiment.

"At that time there was one train running north from Pusan and we loaded up. They hauled everything in those cars and it smelled it. We'd be stopped on occasion, taking incoming rounds. We'd jump into the ditch, fire our weapons, and in a while get back on and be on our way. Some thought it was our guys firing close to the tracks just to indoctrinate us. I don't think so.

"After a few days at a replacement depot, we moved in trucks toward the front. We disembarked about 1 A.M. fifty miles south of the parallel and not too far from the MLR [main line of resistance] and started walking. This bird colonel took charge of the unit to take us up to swap out, man for man, with the on line 24 division.

"I wore or carried everything I owned plus a spool of commo-wire and an ANPRC radio. I had a carbine. I weighed about 140 pounds, and I don't know how much I carried. I kept falling. It was dark except for mortar and artillery fire lighting up the sky. We were scared to death even before we got off that train. We knew what had happened to this outfit in 1950. My gut was in my mouth.

"We take some incoming fire, and I either fall or the blast knocks me down. I'm up then down again and then I don't remember. I wake up and this full bird colonel is slapping my face with his gloves. He's holding both gloves in one hand and popping my face. All I see is the eagle on this damn guy's insignia. 'Get your ass up,' he says, 'C'mon son, you're on me, stay with me,' he says.

"I saw a lot of stuff after that and I was scared to death a good part of the time, but that once was the only time I remember needing a little jumpstart."

★ ★ ★

Kenneth Wilkinson aired one of his own memories. "We marched along a road. There were refugees moving to one side of us. We kept a close eye on them at first but decided they were no problem, just old men and women with packs and pushcarts. We had a South Korean interpreter with us. A few rounds of fairly heavy stuff came in off a good distance then wham! One lands right in the middle of our guys. We hit the deck, and those refugees scatter. In a bit, things quiet down. The locals rise and start walking.

"Our interpreter jumps to his feet and runs to one of those old women. He pulls his pistol and shoots her in the back of the head before anyone can make a move.

"One of our guys hollers. He runs over to the downed woman. She's on her face on the ground, dead. As he nears, the interpreter bends, lifts the woman's shawl or blouse, whatever, and tosses it up and over her head. Beneath it is a radio. Our guy stops, turns, and comes back."

★ ★ ★

Not far from where Larry Zellers heard some of the first shots at Kaesong in 1950, John Washington's hearing tested the quiet after the last firing that followed the armistice signing at Panmunjom in 1953. He had learned to drive tanks at Fort Hood, Texas. In a few weeks he became skilled enough that his country sent him to war. He arrived in Korea in early 1953.

John said, "After a while, they had us move with our tank over to the line near Panmunjom to offer security for the talks and the prisoner exchange. I saw some of those poor guys coming out. Men you could tell had, at one time, weighed 200 pounds were now down to 90 or 100 pounds. You know you're doing something worthwhile when you see that. I was proud to be there.

"We had a 7-power scope mounted on a tripod we looked out over the buffer zone with. A lot of mornings when the talks were going on we'd turn it over to watch both sides arrive for the talks. You may have never heard this before, but as often as not, those officers from both sides would scramble around there duking it out before finally going into the talks."

I stopped writing. "Duking it out, you mean fighting?" I ask.

John made a fist, "That's exactly what I mean, and it didn't just happen once either. We had this old radio. We'd sometimes listen to news reports that night of how cordial and productive the talks had been that day. And there we'd been watching those guy fight it out that morning." He chuckled. "We got a kick out of it."

John's demeanor changed. He looked me in the eye, steady. "But Mackey, we must never see war fought on American soil. And as my daddy said, 'Son, when you can't talk to anybody else, God's available.'"

Chapter 26

Straight to the Top

A soldier mentioned the informality of prayer along the front. "A chaplain came by, you prayed. It didn't matter what day of the week it was, what faith, what denomination he represented. He crawled down in the hole with you and you prayed."

Marine Cpl. Marvin Dunn added, "Almost to a person men prayed to God in combat."

Rev. L. E. Holmes, pastor of the Bethel Baptist Church of Grapevine, Texas, and formerly of the 7th Infantry Division is a veteran of the Chosin Reservoir fighting and four other major campaigns. His born-again Christian salvation occurred after becoming a civilian, but he admits to asking God, "Let me forget the gory stuff."

He showed me a faded, aged, small pocket size testament and said, "My mom sent me this. I carried it with me throughout the war. Oh, I was a moral man, just not saved. I read to the other guys from it and they got comfort, but to me it was just words. He credits the date of December 9, 1956, and Pastor

Bert Rutter of Grand Prairie for preaching the sermon that steered him toward his salvation.

I asked his opinion of the combat scenes and depiction of war portrayed in the movie *Saving Private Ryan*.

"I only watched a portion of it," he explained. "They seemed to have gone overboard on the profanity to me. Men in combat don't use the Lord's name in vain that way. And I found the premise of the army having lost track of a soldier a little unreal."

There may have been a few who failed to call on divine help, but I believe their numbers to be small. I've not met a combat veteran who claimed to be an atheist. Most are unabashedly proud to give credit to a renewed, stronger, more active faith, resulting from a closer proximity to death.

Doc Hughes mentioned placing his dying friend's Bible in the man's weakened hand. He spoke of his own "selfish" prayer as bullets pelted about him, one that asked "Let me live, let me live, God, please let me live."

Wadie Moore told of his prayer for peace for both himself and his buddies. He teetered on the brink, in the midst of death, yet prayed, "God, if you see fit, put me with my buddies in a peaceful place."

Cpl. Dunn said, "It was seven days before I could see again after losing my leg. Shrapnel hit me in the face as well. I prayed, 'God let me live. I'll try to do something to make you proud.' I learned they needed men in teaching. I completed my promise to him."

Mickey Scott received a calming support in the middle of freezing death and destruction. Larry Zellers filled a good portion of his book with stories of prayers from many faiths while a prisoner among the North Koreans. He spoke of his North Korean captors allowing a religious service one distant Christmas Eve.

I am aware of a summer day in August of 1952 that dawned as gray as the bulkhead I leaned against. Fog lay low over the surface of the ground swells running high, as usual, across the shallow Bering Sea. The swells quartered against the flat-bottomed LST, and she rolled in her customary drunken fashion. The sea and sky did a two-step dance up and down in my view, while hook-shaped brackets for a long-lost life ring snuggly held my shoulders against the damp, cold metal of the ship's superstructure.

I was twenty years old, in no immediate danger that I knew of, and had previously crossed those same waters on the way to the Arctic Circle. We were steaming for the Aleutian Islands and then home to the lower States. I'd been out of port three months and felt secure on well-conditioned sea legs and a long ago stable stomach.

I thought of friends I'd left months earlier in the hospital at Corpus Christi and mentally inventoried their disabilities. Scuttlebutt had it that our stay on the West Coast would be brief and that Japan and likely Korea would again be our ship's destination.

Anticipation brought on by the thought of Japan almost outweighed my dread of Korea—almost, but not quite. Had it not been for the reality of Ward 111, I'm sure it would have weighed heavier on the scales.

I looked across the opaque world we sailed and uttered my compromising prayer to God. "God, let me live through this war. And God, afterward let me have just twenty years of knowing what life as a family man, one with a wife and children, is like."

To my discredit, I always bargained with God. Even twenty-three years later in intensive care with a heart attack, I bargained that if he would let me live to the morrow, I'd quit smoking. In spite of my human frailty, he most always comes through. I've not always lived up to my end, however. In the comfort of presumed safety, it seems a human failing to rapidly wander from pledges of even the highest order.

Chapter 26

Glen Thompson said, "Going overseas we thought the rough seas were going to kill us if the enemy didn't. At times, green with seasickness, we almost hoped so. Every night on the main deck there would be these 'street-corner' preachers holding service."

"What kind of preachers?"

"I called them street-corner preachers. Laymen, wanting to relate the heavy stuff they were feeling, I guess. They would have a crowd around them each night." Glen paused.

"You know, coming back, I don't remember seeing a one of those guys." Neither of us speculated further.

Some will disapprove of incidents related in this book and see them as callous or hard, out of step with more refined human values. Many today have matured in a world that allows them to consider all forms of physical conflict inappropriate. Others might remind us that the privilege of living in such an environment has been protected, time and time again, in violent and deadly struggles, not the least of which were borne by Korean War veterans.

Ex-tank driver and Korean War veteran John Washington held me in a steady gaze during an interview shortly after the twin tower disaster in New York. He earlier mentioned his hope and prayer that war never visit the homeland of the United States.

"After Korea I spent some time in Japan. I learned to love nurses there," he said. "I saw some of the results of Hiroshima and Nagasaki. The effects of the blasts, eight or nine years old then, were still horrible to see. More than once, I saw women, nurses, rocking victims of the results of those nuclear explosions. On occasion I saw patients die in their arms. The nurses frequently continued rocking.

A Few Answers—
Many Questions

Recently, I renewed contact with an old friend who saw a lot of the Korean War and came back whole. During one phase of his hitch, he spent time mapping a good part of Korea's terrain. Immediately after the war, before meeting the girl he later married, he logged a few hours plotting cracks and spider webs on the ceiling above his bunk. Like others who served, he'd gathered some hard miles.

I'm unsure if we helped or hindered each other's adjustment to civilian life, but I believe it was mostly positive. Whatever, we shared the experience. We also enjoyed a double date in 1954. The light-hearted activities of the evening culminated in marriage a short time later for both couples. The four of us enjoyed popcorn at the downtown theatre that night.

The movie was a Walt Disney thing, lots of animals, ducks, pretty flowers, and animal antics. It was designed to make you laugh. It used a lot of bright colors, just the thing to help my friend forget the drab winters of Korea. Beautiful mallards glided from flight onto a pond covered with sheet ice they mistook for water. The ducks slid, bowling ball fashion, into each other and created quite a comedy. Disney was a genius. Yet, I believe his wife-to-be taught this private and humble man the fun of laughing again.

I called him in 2001. Over the phone I recognized the lady's voice calling him to my summons. He answered my greeting. I gave him my name and added. "I think I recognize that voice in the background. You mean you two are still together?"

"Good to hear from you. Yeah, that was her."

"It's been a long time. The way things are these days, I was almost afraid to ask. You two are still hitched, then."

"Yeah, we decided to stay until the kids die. I don't know what it is, causes that. Think it's peculiar to our generation." His chuckle came easy.

"I find it that way, also." I replied.

After I got off the phone, I thought of my recent visit with Zuma Hall and her son Art, Bobby Don Hall's widow and son who live in Shreveport, Louisiana.

The first time I called Zuma, I'd already learned that Hall died in 1987. The lady who assisted me in locating his family had found his obituary. After chatting with Zuma and Art awhile, I thought I knew the answer to Bobby Don's question of a half century earlier. I said, "Mrs. Hall, this is awfully personal, but, if I'm going to write this as we've discussed, I need to ask. Did you and Bobby Don have a good marriage?"

I hurriedly continued. "He asked me in 1951, now, his words, not mine. 'Murdock, do you think a fellow like me, a cripple, can find a lady that will love him?'"

Zuma looked at me, her face expressionless. Art sat beside me. His mother's face softened then came alive with feeling.

Bobby Don and Zuma Hall
Photo courtesy of Zuma Hall

Hall would have liked that look. "Mackey, I can assure you he did."

The three of us shared a lot together in their living room that afternoon. Time sort of found reverse for all of us. The more I looked at Art the more he reminded me of his father. Hall's immortality was stamped there.

Art mentioned earlier, "I wish I'd talked more to Dad, asked him more. We talked a lot, but, still..."

I passed on all I knew. I looked at Zuma and reveled in warmth at the knowledge that the young battered but proud friend I'd celebrated life with so many years earlier had fulfilled his quest.

A few days prior to visiting with Zuma and Art, I'd chatted with old friend Mickey Scott. We shared his experiences as a Korean War POW while sitting in a van parked beside a Dairy

Queen in Cleburne, Texas. He told of thirty-two months inching by until the armistice of July 1953 called for a prisoner exchange.

Mickey said, "Teams of six men, supposedly neutral, but actually three from the Communist side and three from the United Nations side came through. They were checking and selecting the most seriously ill men, those missing limbs and/or almost dead, for exchange across the line (38th parallel). It was called 'Operation Little Switch.' A few days later, between July 27th and the 1st of August they started 'Operation Big Switch.' Again, the personnel were determined by a selection process conducted by neutral teams. Some of the guys had to wait a few days. I went out pretty early. I weighed a hundred pounds or less and had about everything imaginable wrong with me.

"I remember getting a USMC utility cap and dress shoes after dismounting from the trucks at Panmunjom. The sight of the U.S. flag was unreal as we reentered life. The first thing, this marine general came to me. He was shaking hands with every marine in that line. He asked the same thing of each of us. 'Do you want anything? Anything at all, son!'

"I said, 'Yes sir, a toothpick.' My teeth were in pretty bad shape. A major could not find a toothpick, so the general had him get a swab and whittle one. Our next stop was with a chaplain."

Larry Zellers was not the chaplain who ministered to Mickey. He still recuperated at that time from his own imprisonment throughout the war in North Korean camps. However he later qualified himself for and served in the air force in that capacity.

Mr. Zeller's missions have, on occasion, returned him to Korea. His book, a documentary journal of his and his companions' struggle for survival, was published in 1991. In his postscript he reports still revisiting Korea on rare occasions in his dreams. At peace, he reports the more violent guards are not present, and in those places where he once barely avoided starvation and death, food is now available. However, there is always one problem. In these gentle, otherwise happy dreams, he is not allowed to go home.

After evacuation from Hungnam, Sergeant Louis Holmes sailed to Pusan. His outfit received brief rest and was re-equipped. By May of 1951 he had made his way back up to the 38th parallel. At that time he rotated home for the first time since 1947. Like Mickey, Holmes associates dental problems with Korea. He blames the water purification tablets he used and his rifle with ruining his teeth.

He said, "Those tablets were hard on your teeth. Mine were a mess when I got home. Of course I only had one tooth-brush over there, and I carried it in the stock of my M-1. I used it for cleaning the working parts of the weapon. It was either my rifle or my teeth."

Bud Archer continued his romance with flying after serving in his two wars, and Sergeant Hardy Richards fulfilled his desire to improve on the agribusiness of feeding America. Almost to a man those who I followed up on utilized the G.I. Bill to improve their marketability and productivity. In my judgment, its availability is one of those things for which our country should be proud.

I've not found the young marine Pruitt, who provided me with a lifetime philosophy that makes labeling the living with the title hero so difficult. I hold onto hope of meeting him again. Perhaps, if it occurs, it is meant to be a private matter.

Doc Hughes still runs and is fit. Today he jogs on the track around the university were he taught so many years. The hill where his home is located is a quiet place. The air is free of incoming sounds of war, and no projectiles whine overhead. Currently, his battles are confined to an occasional attack on leaves wafting onto the surface of his pool.

Clarence Archer in later years.
Photo courtesy of C. Archer

We spoke of age and agreed it offered opportunity for courage. We generalized about life over sixty-five and searched for a positive note to end such a fruitless subject.

Always the linguist, Charlie summed it up: "Old age isn't for sissies."

Bill Mackey, Carl Kisinger, and I returned to college after the war. We ran together again, had some laughs, and somehow managed to graduate. We didn't go visit Dean Woods to tell him we made it back. We probably thought he'd not remember us, anyway. We had to have something to feel a little abused about, some reason to justify a trip to the bar in Saginaw.

The ranks of those who returned from Korea are thinning some now. Not nearly at the rate of loss of those vicious three years, but time takes a toll. My ship sailed to the South Pacific

Hardie and Betty Richards taken during the H Co. 3rd Bn. 7 Marine Reunion
(Korea Veterans), at Branson, Missouri 2001.
Photo courtesy of H.L. Richards

Chapter 27

Bill and Carol Mackey enjoying new adventures in New Mexico.

after the war. I hear from some of the guys. The crew of later days participated in the nuclear tests conducted after Korea. The guys who follow that sort of thing provide a sort of crew's obituary. A separate listing is reserved for those with a cause of death identified as "radiation sickness."

Thank goodness, time indicates John O'Callaghan escaped such a fate in spite of his stint near testing in Nevada. It appears others, in the Pacific, may not have.

It's comforting to know, down I-20 a few miles, ole Tex Owens still holds to his sense of humor. He started one story with, "You can choke me if it ain't true," and chuckled easily as he told it. I can't imagine anyone choking Tex Owens.

I found the answer to Bobby Don Hall's question. Zuma put the lid on that one. Love does conquer physical disability.

The guys on the *Ulvert M. Moore* and the USS *Renshaw* may never know the identity of their quarry in the Yellow Sea. Was it a Russian sub?

Wadie Moore asked the lights that were shining in his face, "Am I gonna make it?"

From the darkness behind the lights came a reply from a Catholic priest then a Jewish rabbi, "We can't tell you."

Wadie prayed for himself and his family. He instructed God, "If you see fit, put me in a peaceful place with my buddies."

Time gave us the answer to Wadie's question, and God delivered on the prayer. Each time the "Fighting 7th" of the 1st Marine Division has a conference, a reunion, Wadie is there. He's trim, striking in his dress blues. A quiet and elegant lady whose name he changed from Henderson to Moore is not far away. From her attention to Wadie the day we chatted, I believe she still finds an attraction in dress blue.

In Ennis, Texas, Carl Cope, World War II pilot, brother to MIA Captain Troy Gordon Cope, continues to ask his questions. "What was Gordy's fate? Was he captured, sent to Russia? Did he meet a swift death? Is he alive today?" Captain Gordon Cope's three sons, Johnny, Danny, and Mike echo the question.

When all hands are mustered on that final quarterdeck, perhaps the Old Man charting our new course will answer the remaining questions. I bet there will be some grizzled old uncles, dads, maybe an older brother or two from the "Big One" there. Maybe some of those salty but bright-eyed kids from more recent conflicts.

There'll be a bunch from this new generation. They'll have many civilians among them, firemen, police, secretaries, everyday workers of all descriptions who witnessed and reacted to the horror of terrorism in New York. I look forward to the chance to salute that bunch.

Biographies

ARCHER, CAPTAIN "BUD" CLARENCE, U.S. Army Air Force Pilot. Interview August 7, 2001, Irving, Texas.

Bud Archer was born November 21, 1924, in Okolona, Mississippi. At that time his birthplace was a terminal for the Mobile and Ohio Railroad. The son of a railroad worker, Bud's interest turned to a lighter version of cutting-edge technology. He became enchanted with airplanes.

A visit to Fort Worth, Texas, on Pearl Harbor Day, 1941 foreshadowed both his later career and soon-to-be home state. Archer entered the Army Air Force at Camp Shelby, Mississippi in 1943. He was determined to become a pilot despite what he called his own "buckteeth." "All the men's pictures on military posters had even teeth," he said.

Lieutenant Archer flew B-24s while stationed with the 8th Air Force in Norwich, England during the last year of World War II. His wing commander at that time was Jimmy Stewart of Hollywood fame. He quoted Stewart's reply to the wing's maintenance officer's request for sixty plane engines. "We'll order one hundred and twenty-five, maybe we'll get the sixty."

Clarence returned to civilian life for a short period after World War II then was recalled during the Korean War. During that period he flew C-47 transports in North Africa and C-119 troop carriers in Europe and the Near East. His main base of operation was the 1603 Air Transport Wing, Wheelus Air Force Base, Tripoli, Libya. His missions included the supply of radar installations along the coast of North Africa as well as troop movement and air supply throughout that part of the world.

Lieutenant Archer, later Captain Archer, saw duty at almost every imaginable army and/or air force base in Texas. He started at the Army Cadet School (Lackland) in San Antonio in 1943 and at various times served at Primary Flying School (Gibb's Field), Fort Stockton, Texas; basic training at Goodfellow Field, San Angelo; and advanced training, multi-engine, at Pampa, Texas.

In 1947 he married Mildred Mathis of Okolona, Mississippi, and they raised five children. Today he and his wife reside in Irving, Texas.

His most memorable flying experience—winning a half-crown bet that the plane he flew in crashed before making the runway in England. It was Hitler's birthday, April 21, 1944, in Norwich, England. He survived the crash but lost his watch in his haste to evacuate the plane. A month later his watch was returned to him by mechanics assigned to cannibalize the aircraft for parts. He doesn't remember receiving payment for the bet.

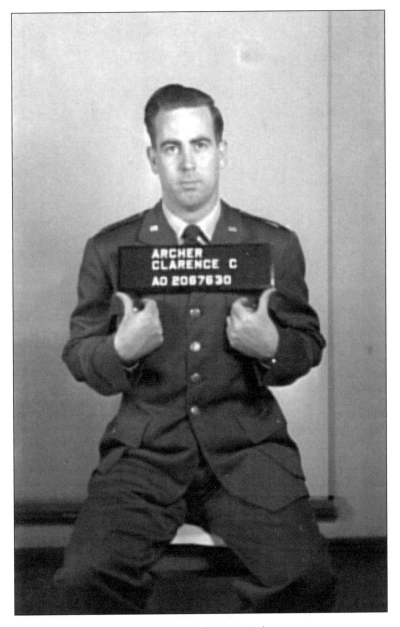

Captain "Bud" Clarence Archer.
Photo courtesy of Clarence Archer

BUCKMAN, ED, U.S. Navy Airman (Electronics Tech), flight deck crew USS *Princeton* (CV-37). Interviewed October 2, 2001, Hurst, Texas.

Born December 1, 1929, Ed spent his twenty-first birthday on duty and confined to his ship amidst the pungent odor of Sasebo, Japan. His birthplace was Norristown, Pennsylvania. "My claim to fame is growing up in the same neighborhood with Tommy Lasorda of L.A. Dodger fame. I used to chase baseballs he hit into the local creek," he said.

Ed's ship, the *Princeton*, a part of Air Group Nineteen, lists fourteen lost pilots in Korean waters. Some Ed knew better than others, all were his shipmates. After the war, he married Jody Rowlett of El Reno, Oklahoma.

Ed said, "I was discharged in 1952. I had a cushy time of it compared to many over there, a warm bunk and good chow. But I didn't mention Korea until 1995 when they built the memorial. Shortly after that I discovered a lot of declassified records. I helped a nephew of a lost pilot get the flight log pertaining to his uncle's last flight. Since then I've stayed pretty busy with it.

"We went to the National Parade in New York in 2000 for the Veteran's Day celebration. I went to pay homage to the thousands who never came back. Mackey, there were one million grateful citizens on 5th Avenue that day. I have been active in veteran affairs since that time. It made a change in my life. I wish you had been there."

I wish I had. This guy, the pilots he served, and the ship he helped man were responsible for tearing up a lot of communist turf. Later known as the "bridge busters," they also provided air support for the escape route from the Chosin Reservoir that allowed many soldiers and marines to live to fight another day.

Ed Buckman
Photo courtesy of Ed Buckman

COPE, CAPT. TROY GORDON "GORDY," (Missing In Action) USAF 335th Fighter Interceptor Squadron, 4th Fighter Interceptor Group, APO 970. Interviewed his brother, Carl Cope, September 7, 2001, Ennis, Texas.

Carl handed me an official air force declassified document dealing with his brother's missing flight. "Circumstances: Flight was attacked by MiGs Sept. 16, 1952—pilot was last seen at 30,000 ft. aprox 5 miles south of Sinuiuu near the Yalu River. Last radio transmission heard was that pilot believed he had 3 MiGs in sight. Believed down in enemy territory. Information from "Unclassified" Attachment #1 to AFFm 484, Auth: CO, 4th Ftr-Intp Wg. Rec. and provided by Carl Cope of Ennis, Texas. (Re-graded July 1, 1955—declassified at a later date.)

The *Dallas Morning News* on Tuesday, June 26, 2001, ran a story about this missing airman headed "Piece Of The Puzzle." It states, "About five years ago, Mr. Cope [Carl] learned that a businessman had returned from a visit to China with rubbings of American dog tags, including the captain's [Gordy Cope's] that he found in a Korean War Memorial Museum. The museum was in Dandong, China, near where Capt. Cope was reported lost."

Captain Troy Cope is the father of three sons, Johnny, Danny, and Mike. They have grown to manhood without knowing their dad. Their Uncle Carl and his wife, Marion, have done all possible to bridge that void. Captain Cope's plane went down with "Rosie," his wife's name, painted on its side.

Carl Cope was born in Mountain Home, Arkansas, in 1921. Gordy was born two years later in 1923. Carl remembers a "hillbilly" childhood of swimming, squirrel hunting, a younger brother hollering, "Wait for me," and lazy hours along Arkansas' White River.

Each brother served in the Army Air Force in World War II, Carl as a troop carrier (C-47) pilot in the Mediterranean and Gordy as a fighter pilot in Alaska. Both ultimately achieved the

Captain Troy Gordon Cope

rank of captain. Carl spoke of crash landing in an olive grove in Sicily after being hit by, perhaps, friendly fire in 1942.

He said Gordy was called to active duty during the Korean War and gone before they had a chance at a proper goodbye. Carl provided me with a seventy-seven-page ALL POW-MIA Transfer report. It states under EXECUTIVE SUMMARY, "U.S. Korean War POWs were transferred to the Soviet Union and never repatriated." Page 17 of Part 11 lists Captain Cope as one of thirty-one missing USAF F-86 pilots whose loss indicates possible capture and later transfer to the Soviet Union. The brief description of his loss says:

"19. Pilot: Captain Troy G. Cope, USAFR, Date of Casualty: 16 September 1952, Status: MIA.

"After several encounters with enemy fighter aircraft while participating in a fighter sweep operation along the Yalu, Captain Cope radioed that his ammunition was exhausted. Accompanied by another flight member he headed downstream on a course south of the Manchurian border and parallel to the Yalu. Approximately 10 miles south of Antung, two flights of MiGs were sighted and, while maneuvering to attack, the accompanying pilot noticed three other enemy aircraft in the area. He promptly radioed this information to Captain Cope who acknowledged the message. Because of the prevailing conditions, the two F-86s became separated. Efforts to re-establish visual or radio contact with Captain Cope were unsuccessful. An extensive aerial search revealed no traces of Captain Cope or his aircraft."

The name of the businessman who brought rubbings from his brother's dog tags has not been revealed to Mr. Cope. His interest in making the story available springs from the faint hope that after fifty years some light might be shed on the details of his missing brother's fate. I share that hope.

DUNN, CORPORAL MARVIN, 1st Provisional Marine Brigade, 1st Regiment, 1st Battalion, Able Co. Interviewed October 8, 2001, Arlington, Texas.

Born May 4, 1931, in Wichita Falls, Texas, Marvin Dunn spent his childhood on a farm near Paris, Texas. He married Jo Ann Morris from that community on December 20, 1952. They continue to share life together today.

The first thing one notices when meeting Marvin is his neatness of dress. Later, when talking of his childhood on a farm in the thirties, he admitted to always loving nice clothes.

"I always wanted more than one pair of clothes a year," he said. He looks good in those clothes today, coordinated, trim, and well conditioned.

It was only after he mentioned the loss of his lower leg in Korea that I became aware of his prosthesis. The official record states he stepped on a mine. "I don't think so," he said. "I believe to this day I heard it coming in. I think I even hollered, 'look out!' I was carrying logs to build a bunker; they absorbed a lot of shrapnel, saved my life, I believe."

Dunn didn't make it down to the U.S. naval hospital at Corpus Christi. He received his stateside, continuing in-service medical care at the Amputee Ward of the Naval Hospital, Oakland, California. Determined to continue his life as near unrestricted as possible, he continues to enjoy most forms of physical activity.

Blinded for a number of days by the blast that took his lower leg, Corporal Dunn said, "I promised God if he let me live, I'd try to do something to make him proud. I later entered the teaching field and recently retired from the Dallas public school system."

Marvin and Jo Ann have two daughters and five grandchildren. Hundreds, probably thousands of students no doubt benefited from his promise.

Hall, CORPORAL BOBBY DON, 1st Marines, 7th Regiment, 1st Battalion, C Company. I shared a hospital ward for five months in 1951 with Hall. Interviewed his widow and son April 2001, Shreveport, Louisiana.

Bobby Don Hall was born in Marshall, Texas, on February 8, 1929. A corporal when I knew him, Hall wrote to his home in Marshall from Korea on April 21, 1951. Shortly after that he had a kneecap destroyed by enemy fire. Bobby Don died January 9, 1987, from heart failure.

During his marine hitch, he departed Camp Pendleton on November 15, 1950, then disembarked from San Diego for Korea aboard the transport *General E. T. Collins*. He later told his wife he and a buddy toasted the fading California shoreline from the fantail of their vessel with a smuggled bottle of booze to the tune of the day, "Harbor Lights." He arrived in Masan, Korea December 18, 1950.

After his injury and discharge from the marines he met then married Zuma Carrie Bays, who later presented him with their child, Art. The lady who proved to Hall that, though he was a casualty, a woman's love would surround his postwar days, brought me up to date on Art's birth. Zuma recalled with love and perhaps a touch of wifely resentment that Bobby Don and her doctor talked duck hunting while she delivered the baby. According to her, she and Bobby Don counted the child's fingers and toes then their blessings.

Many brave men fought under a number of national flags for the United Nation's forces in Korea. Corporal Hall made sure the flag of his home state also flew over those bloody grounds. He requested the Lone Star flag of Texas and his father, a World War I veteran, obtained and mailed one to Korea. Perhaps some veteran will remember seeing it waving in that far-away land. Zuma and Art showed it to me at their home in Shreveport in 2001. Marine combat-boot laces were still attached to its grommets.

Bobby Don Hall
Photo courtesy of Zuma Hall

HOLMES, SERGEANT 1ST CLASS LOUIS E., U.S. Army, 7th Infantry Division, 31st Regiment, 2nd Battalion, Co. E. Interviewed October 11, 2001, Grapevine, Texas.

Sergeant Holmes was born October 23, 1930, in East St. Louis, Illinois. At an early age his family moved to Benton, Illinois. In February of 1948 he and a cousin talked their respective parents into signing for them to join the army in Waco, Texas. He was sworn in at Love Field in Dallas, Texas, and attended basic training at Fort Ord, California.

Holmes performed well as a soldier and was recognized for his effort and ability. His platoon leader selected him to represent his company in Leadership School. He graduated at the top of his class and on May 20, 1950, was selected as an army representative for the first Armed Forces Day celebration. At that time he was in Japan.

The ex-sergeant doesn't buy the tag "soft peacetime military." Later assigned as an instructor in Leadership School, he maintains that much of the military was hard, well trained, and ready when ROK and replacement personnel necessarily flooded in after the onslaught of the war to dilute the overall preparedness. Their readiness, equipment, and manpower became simply overwhelmed.

Holmes landed in Inchon, Korea during the invasion and later moved to find himself engaged on the east side of the reservoir. He fought at Hagaru-ri down to Koto-ri and was ultimately evacuated at Hungnam.

For three years Holmes had engaged in an almost daily pen-pal relationship with Edna Holt of Oklaunion, Texas. They never met until he came home in May of 1951. They knew, however, they were in love, where they wanted to live, the kind of home and life they wanted, and the number of children they felt would be ideal. They saw each other on Wednesday and were married on Sunday. He calls her Kitten, a nickname given her after their wedding. Today they have two children, Louis

Louis E. Holmes
Photo courtesy of L.E. Holmes

and Jeanne, complemented by five grandchildren. They recently celebrated their fiftieth anniversary.

The planned occupation as an oilrig driller came to pass for a while near Electra, Texas. Then he answered a higher calling. On September 16, 1962, Louis became pastor at Bethel Baptist Church in Grapevine, Texas, and has been there since that time.

HUGHES, CHARLES "DOC" W., U.S. Navy Hospital Corps-man assigned to H Company, 3rd Battalion, 7th Regiment, 1st Platoon, 1st Marine Division. Interviewed September 5, 2001, Arkadelphia, Arkansas.

Born July 24, 1931, in Dallas, Texas, Charles waited one month after his seventeenth birthday before dropping out of school to join the navy in August 1948. He preferred the coast guard, but they were only taking enlistees one at a time and since a buddy wanted to go with him, they chose the navy.

When asked his first three choices for rating preference after boot camp, the apprentice seaman listed submarines, gun-ners mate, and then hesitated for his third choice. The petty officer with the pencil supplied hospital corpsman. Hughes soon found himself stationed at Oak Knoll Naval Hospital at Oakland, California.

In 1950 Oak Knoll began to receive its first wounded from Korea, mostly marines. Anxious for adventure, Hughes and friend Ollen Langston requested assignment to the Fleet Marine Force. Days later they were training with the Marine Corps at Camp Pendleton, California. Doc Hughes spent nine months in Korean combat with the marines. In his words, he prayed "selfishly" for his own life a number of times while going to the aid of or working feverishly to save others. His prayers were answered.

Charles returned to Texas and on August 23, 1958, married Elsie Marie Voyles. They raised two children, Cyndi and Chuck. He answered informally, but proudly, to Doc in Korea. After earning a Bachelor of Arts from the University of Texas, a Mas-ter of Arts and a Doctor of Philosophy from Texas Tech University, Doctor became his official title.

A gifted writer, Charles has published poetry, short stories, and essays. For the last thirty years he and Marie have made their home in Arkadelphia, Arkansas, where he found fulfillment in his chosen career as Professor of English at Henderson State University. Getting to know Charles Hughes is one of the many rare pleasures life has dealt me.

Charles and Marie Hughes
H-3-7 reunion; Branson, Missouri (Spring 2001)
Photo courtesy of Charles Hughes

KISINGER, CARL JR., AET3, U.S. Navy. Served aboard the USS *Essex* (CV-9), the USS *Antietam* (CV-36) and the USS *Yorktown*. Interviewed September 2001, Seymour, Texas. A treasured friend before and after the Korean War.

Kisinger saw action in Korean waters and heard the dreaded words "Man overboard" from his ship's squawk boxes as both flight deck crewmen and pilots were lost at sea.

Carl was born May 14, 1931, in Red Springs, Texas. His father farmed and his mother taught school. He married Sybil Reid after the war in 1955 and they were blessed with four children. After graduating from college, Carl worked for and retired from the Sperry-Sun Co. Today he and Sybil have returned to Carl's hometown of Seymour to enjoy their later years.

Mackey, William K., IC1, U.S. Navy, USS *Ulvert M. Moore* (DE-442). Interviewed 1953, 1954, and by phone in 2001, Abiquiu, New Nexico.

Bill Mackey was born in Norton, Texas. He served in the U.S. Navy at the end of World War II then volunteered to go back into active duty during the Korean War. Always one with a knack for gravitating toward the unusual, Bill found himself on liberty in the greatest liberty town of them all on VJ Day—The Big Easy—New Orleans.

Following the war and in the lackluster days of peacetime, a greatly reduced and relaxed navy sent veterans home and left the highest noncom in charge of many assignments in the South Pacific. Bill soon found himself in command of a half-dozen or so enlisted crewmen and a landing craft tank. At the time he was still in his teens, and the ship's orders were to lay low with few formal duties except bask in the sun and peaceful waters around the Philippine Islands. An LCT is not an ocean going vessel, but it is adequate for island jumping and will carry a few tanks or a lot of beer.

In those slow dog days following the end of WW II, booze was a major item on the LCT's requisition list so Bill had no problem conditioning himself to run with me in college. We did just that in 1949 and 1950 then again after Korea in 1953-4.

The navy and Korea were a little more active for Bill than the days following WW II. He found himself dodging fire from shore batteries, dropping depth charges on, most likely, somebody's submarine, and in a rare moment of insanity, acting as a forward observer for the USS *Missouri*'s big guns.

Bill honed his wedding skills performing as my best man in 1954 then convinced his girlfriend, Carol, to join him in matrimony in 1955. During his college days he found time to become president of the student government at North Texas State College, now the University of North Texas. He earned a B.S. degree in Industrial Arts.

Bill Mackey

Bill and Carol enjoyed a number of years in industry, raised two children, and today enjoy a state of semiretirement, hosting guests at the Presbyterian Ghost Ranch conference center in New Mexico. Unselfish, intelligent, and loyal, good friend Bill, like so many of his counterparts, never failed muster when his country called.

MCGILL, BILL, EN3, U.S. Navy, USS LST-1146. Interviewed September 18, 2001, by phone, Searcy, Arkansas.

McGill was born February 28, 1932, in Tyler, Texas. He joined the navy at an early age. We served aboard the same ship for a period of time during the Korean conflict. A nonsmoker when smoking was cool, McGill promised his father he'd never smoke. At age twenty-one he still lived by that promise. He displayed a ready smile.

On their way to Korea aboard the USS 1146 the crew was encouraged to make out their will. In 2001 Bill recalled the document's contents: "I left my uniform to one brother and the 45 RPM records to another. I put the thing [will] in my locker, never thinking if it became needed, chances were, the ship would be on the bottom of the ocean," Bill laughed.

Bill loves music, the sound of heavy diesel engines, and most of all giving of himself to family, his church members, and the many children he has sponsored through life.

Miller, SERGEANT ED, 4th Battery, 11th Regiment, 1st
Marine Div. Interviewed October 10, 2001, Frisco, Texas.

Miller was born in Texarkana, Texas, May 21, 1930. "I lost
my father when I was two. With the insurance money, my
mother purchased one city block of land near downtown
Texarkana. I remember chickens and okra, a lot of each," Ed
said.

A local businessman, the owner of Lavender Radio, an electronics parts distributor, took Ed, as a youngster, under his
wing and provided a father-figure image. The man sat Miller at
a desk near his own and involved him in every aspect of his
business. A short time afterwards the owner placed a section of
rope across his desk. He said, "Here's a piece of rope; you can
hang yourself or climb to the top. Don't say anything; come
back tomorrow and tell me which it will be."

The next day Ed responded, "Okay, I'm ready to climb to
the top." He did just that and before the age of twenty was running the man's business consisting of stores in Tyler, Little
Rock, and various other locations.

"I was his hatchet man," Ed said. "I hired, fired, and in general had full authority."

In 1948 Ed joined the U.S. Marine Reserves for "a trip to
California and $64 a quarter." On July 25, 1950, at the age of
twenty, he married Jean Johnson and three days later received
orders to active duty.

Miller says he saw little in the way of leadership or worthwhile information coming from the marine noncoms used to
prepare his group for combat after their arrival in California.
"You got to understand, at this point I have an ego of fifteen on
a scale of ten."

Fifty-four out of the one hundred and fifty-four of his acti-
vated group were sent to Korea. Ed found himself among the
fifty-four. There, he learned that those noncoms he had looked
down on, in fact, provided him with his only chance for survival.

Sergeant Ed Miller
Photo courtesy Ed Miller

That knowledge came from "a series of traumatic experiences that taught me the value in every man, and that we all have to find and utilize our strengths while learning to make adjustments."

Sergeant Miller never had the benefit of boot camp. "After being called up from the reserves, I learned to field strip my weapon aboard the USS *Henry S. Weigel* en route to Korea." He went ashore during the Inchon invasion then later moved back to the east coast of Korea and bypassed the mine infested harbor of Hungnam to disembark a few miles up the coast. His battery made it north "on an icy pass you wouldn't believe." He fought at Yudam-ni, then at Koto-ri a round grazed his helmet. Near Hagaru-ri an American truck ran over his legs, leaving him temporarily unable to walk. He was one of the last casualties thrown aboard a C-46 for evacuation.

Ed spent thirty-seven days in Japan, five of them in the hospital, before volunteering to go back to Korea. He was the third man rotated home to the States from his battalion in June of 1951.

Today Ed runs his own company and devotes much of his time to the Korean War veteran's organization known as the Chosin Few. His purpose now as in Korea is to help his comrades who made up an elite group of fighting men and served their country during the months of November and December 1950 in the Chosin Reservoir area of North Korea. Short of another round to the helmet, a shower of shrapnel, and being run over by a deuce-and-a-half, I expect him to man that post for some time.

MOORE, SERGEANT WADIE, Howe Company, 7th Regiment, 1st Marine Division. Interviewed August 3, 2001, Commerce, Texas.

Sergeant Moore was born in Delta County, Texas, on July 23, 1932. Impatient for life, Wadie struggled into this world early. Weighing only two pounds, he seemed near death so the doctor used "Baby" on the birth certificate to spare his grieving mother the trauma of selecting a name. After all, its only use would be for a death certificate. Cribbed in a shoebox, Moore fooled them and lived. Eighteen years later it took "a stalk of bananas and a gallon of water" to get him over the minimum weight limit of 118 pounds to enlist in the U.S. Marine Corps. Small even in maturity, his spirit, the will to fight and survive, is immense.

Moore made a good marine. What he lacked in size he made up for in energy, spunk, and desire—ingredients the marines knew how to utilize. In early summer of 1951 he found himself in Korea. A few months later he faced his last enemy guns on a piece of Korea the marines called "The Punch Bowl." His battle for life and recovery lasted years.

Missing an eye and with a large hole where it, his nose, and part of his head had been, Wadie Moore said a prayer for himself and his family. His request was simple. "God, if you see fit, put me in a peaceful place with my buddies." A buddy's instructions; a black man's voice from the blindness surrounding him, "Doc" Willie Stewart; Korean "Blue Boys" who ultimately dropped him in the river; a sergeant directing helicopter evacuations; and his own tenacity were all utilized in implementing his prayer's answer.

A young navy surgeon named Joseph R. Connelly, ultimately Commander Connelly, was the instrument used in helping time put him physically and mentally back together. The immediate spiritual change he described as "a transformation from the hell that was going on to a feeling of peace and quiet that I've never experienced before and probably never will again," stands on its own.

The only thing stronger than the bond that grew between Moore and Commander Connelly was the love the sergeant developed for a hometown girl named Norma Jean Henderson. They were married October 23, 1952. Wadie stayed under the doctor's care for three years. He's been under Norma Jean's a half-century. Medically retired from the marines, Buck Sergeant Wadie Moore became Ph.D. Wadie Moore, professor of English and Linguistics at the University of A&M at Commerce, Texas. He and Norma Jean raised two children, Kevin and Quinn.

O'CALLAGHAN, CPL. JOHN J. III, U.S. Marines, C Company, 3rd Regiment, 3rd Div. (unformed). Interviewed June 20, 2001, Irving, Texas.

O'Callaghan was born in Memphis, Tennessee, February 21, 1931. John enlisted in the U.S. Marine Corps on February 5, 1951. He was stationed at Camp Fuji, Gotemba, Japan, and Camp Pendleton, Calif. On February 5, 1954, he received his discharge. Like many wartime veterans, he was never assigned to a combat theater.

He said, "It doesn't sound very patriotic, but a friend, familiar with the draft board sequence, called. She said, 'John, in three weeks you're going to be drafted.' Well, I didn't want the army, and the air force and navy both had four-year enlistment, so I joined the marines for three years."

I met John during a book signing. As I signed the book, I mentioned working on another book covering the Korean War period and interviewing ex-servicemen of that era.

John said, "I was in the marines during that time but was not in combat. We fought some fires out West, did a lot of training, then shipped over to Japan." He thanked me for the book and mentioned as he turned to walk away, "I did see three nuclear devices set off, though."

I had never knowingly talked to a man who witnessed an atomic explosion. "When can I come to your house and talk?" I asked.

The testing he witnessed was performed in Nevada in 1953. His closest distance to ground zero at the time of any of the explosions was two and a half miles. The others were seen from ten to fifteen miles. "For protection we and other observers had a six-foot-deep trench and were told to look down," he said. The marines' mission there was to serve as guards and be available for later radiation contamination testing.

John married Dixie Lee Brewer. They moved to Texas in 1969 and raised two children, a boy and a girl. After the service

John worked as a heavy truck mechanic and shop foreman. He and Dixie make their home in Irving, Texas. To his knowledge, he's suffered no ill effects from his exposure.

John O'Callaghan (1951)
Photo courtesy of John O'Callaghan

OWENS, CHARLES ARTHUR "TEX," EC2, U.S. Navy, USS LST-1146. (Shipmates two years.) Interviewed September 4, 2001, in Longview, Texas.

"Tex" Owens was born January 13, 1931, on a farm near Gilmer, Texas. That event qualified him as the third generation of his family to be born on that plot of ground. Shortly after joining the U.S. Navy he met and married Lillie Maude Allen on October 1, 1951.

Owens was my shipmate, a good sailor and an excellent mechanic. He served one tour with the USS LST-1146 in Korea and participated in the invasion of Inchon. After his return from Japan and Korea, he made at least two supply runs deep into the Arctic in support of our country's Defense Early Warning strategy.

With his wife, Maude, he spent his years after the war in Longview, Texas. He retired from the Longview Fire Department.

RICHARDS, STAFF SERGEANT HARDIE LEE, H Company, 3rd Battalion, 7th Regiment, 1st Marine Division. Interviewed (phone) June 14, 2001, Idaho Falls, Idaho. (Recuperated together five months in Ward 111, USN Air Station Hospital, Corpus Christi, Texas, 1951.)

Staff Sergeant Hardie Lee Richards was born November 8, 1926, in Vera, Texas. His family farmed. It was a way of life he was comfortable with. After graduation from high school, Hardie Lee served his first hitch in the marines. It was 1945 and World War II required young men. At the time the atomic bombs were dropped, he had received his training and was en route to the Pacific Theatre. An unthinkable invasion of Japan loomed as his outfit's ultimate destination.

Spared by the war's end, Richards attended Texas A&M University. Still in the marine reserve, he found himself recalled to active duty when things got hot in Korea in the last half of 1950.

At the time the marines recalled Hardie Lee, he pursued a fragmented plan. His farm upbringing told him there had to be an economic way of putting weight on farm animals, "finish them out," that was more efficient than current methods. He had some kinks to work out, details to move around, skills to learn, but he'd get there. He'd make it work. This new war that almost killed him had not been part of the program, but all who knew him had no doubt that it nor the wound it dealt him would long delay his course.

He worked at physical therapy harder than most to regain his abilities. He carried himself with pride and held the respect of all who knew him. I'm no expert on marines, but at the risk of sounding corny, in my judgment he was a marine's marine, a leader others followed willingly.

In 1952 he married Betty Inman. Betty grew up in Vinita, Oklahoma. Somehow Richards must have fooled her. When he

Hardie L. Richards
Photo courtesy of Hardie Richards

answered the phone in Idaho in 2001 to talk to me, she was still by his side. They raised three boys: Ronnie, Tony, and Steve.

During our second phone conversation, after being fifty years out of touch, Richards said, "I've been thinking about you since you called. I remember we called you the 'The Kid,' didn't we?"

"Probably. I'll take that now," I answered. I shifted the conversation and asked about his later occupation.

"Animal nutrition. I went back and got more schooling then worked for a company in the field. In later years I joined some other guys, and we put together the first hog feedlot in Idaho using potato byproducts as part of the feed ration," he said.

Richard's wound entered in the area of the collarbone, pierced a lung, broke some bone, and exited out his back. In the hospital, marines referred to him, not by his first name, but as "Staff Sergeant Richards." Kid sailors did likewise.

SCOTT, STAFF SERGEANT MICKEY K., Dog Co., 2nd Battalion, 7th Marine Regiment of the 1st Marine Division. Interviewed March 21, 2001, Cleburne, Texas.

Mickey was born August 3, 1928, in Hamlin, Texas. From the age of ten he had one goal—to become a "leatherneck"—a United States Marine. Eighteen years to the day after his birth, he graduated from the Marine Corps Recruit Depot at San Diego, California. The year was 1946. He'd had to take things into his own hands a bit by playing hooky and hitchhiking to Abilene, Texas, on the last school day of his junior year to enlist. That decision helped set up difficulty for Mickey, but he's still proud of his service and the marines.

Mickey, like many other stateside marines, volunteered to go to the assistance of U.S. forces in Korea in 1950. His outfit, Dog Co., 2nd Battalion, 7th Marine Regiment of the 1st Division, fought their way to the Chosin Reservoir. Soon he and two buddies found themselves surrounded by an army of Chinese. Cut off from support from other members of their company, they were taken prisoner by the Communist Chinese.

He said, "For years I felt, with a strange calmness, that I actually died that day near a little hamlet named Kyodong-ni."

The night following his capture was the 27th of November 1950; the night the communists attacked the 1st Marines Division that was dug in at Yudam-ni, Hagaru-ri, and Koto-ri. Mickey spent that night and most of the next three years as a prisoner of the Communist Chinese. The fight continued to Hamhung on the Yellow Sea.

After returning to life across the thirty-eighth parallel, Mickey said, "They put us on the USS *Hase*, a transport, equipped with good medical staff and facilities. When we landed stateside it was an immediate thirty-day leave for those whose physical condition allowed it, then to the hospital for tests and treatment. I spent about thirty days in the Naval Air Station

Hospital at Corpus Christi, Texas, but I don't remember which ward I was in."

Mickey was discharged in 1953 then transferred to Marine Corps Reserve for four years. He took a year off and did nothing, if you can call adjusting to civilian life after thirty months in a Communist Chinese prison nothing. He was home in Hamlin, in his words, a little aggressive and belligerent. "When you hold in that much hurt and anger for over two and a half years without humor or smiling at least some, it's a little tough to snap out of."

When Mickey mentioned doing nothing, I knew he'd finally arrived at my area of expertise. That was the main theatre I'd served in. I nodded knowingly. "Hit the bottle some, did you?" I asked.

Mickey gave me one of those looks. I think it said, "There's a limit to where we go with this." He later denied that thought.

Resolved to make sure he did not burn out this time, Mickey returned to Hardin Simmons University at Abilene in 1954 and obtained a B.B.A. in business then an M.A. in economics. While a student he met and married Barbara Holcombe from Abilene. They raised two children and at this writing have been married for forty-five "magnificent" years. They reside in Cleburne, Texas.

In 1957 Mickey left the corps for his final time as a staff sergeant. His contribution of eleven and a half years to his corps and to his country are only surpassed by the lifetime of honor and devotion he served his fellow men. He endured some of the most outrageous conditions man has ever suffered, but still he retains his love for his country and the spirit of a marine. In his words, "Once a marine, always a marine."

When I interviewed Mickey, three decades had passed since we supervised the same assembly line on different shifts for Texas Instruments, Inc. We worked together during the 1960s.

Mickey said, "After nearly fifty years the government sent three more medals and ribbons."

It was good to see Mickey. We didn't have a beer. I'm not sure if he touches it. Come to think of it, he refused my offer of bottled water. Still, remembering his days in captivity without it, I'm glad I offered.

Mickey K. Scott
Photo courtesy of Mickey Scott

SMITH, SERGEANT CHARLES, U.S. Army, M Co. (Heavy Weapons) 224th Infantry Regiment, 40th Division. Interviewed October 2, 2001, Arlington, Texas.

Charles Smith was born January 18, 1927, in Burnet, Texas. His family farmed. Charles said, "My first eight years of school were in a two-room schoolhouse, and I never moved from the same seat and desk."

Like so many inland sons, the sea seemed an exciting place, and he joined the Merchant Marines in 1944 and took his first cruise to the South Pacific. In the next few years he washed away the monotony of the consistent view from that childhood desk with voyages that carried him to many of the world's ports on different oceans and seas. For a kid who kept the same seat for eight years, he saw a lot of the world in the next five.

After the war he returned to Burnet and married Johnnie Marie Burk. The wedding took place on June 3, 1949. In business, in debt, and in love, he never expected to be drafted, but that is exactly what happened to him in 1952. The Korean War raged, and earlier service in the Merchant Marines at that time earned no military service recognition. To compound his misery, a law was implemented authorizing delay of payment of debts by servicemen, and the banks shut off most loans to draftees. Charles took a beating on his business.

Smith saw a lot of action in Korea, much of which escapes his memory today. He was discharged from active duty January 6, 1954. He stayed in the reserve until 1960 and left the service as a master sergeant. Today he lives in Arlington, Texas, and stays active assisting other veterans and taking a proactive position on veteran affairs.

Corporal Charles C. Smith
224th Regiment
40th Division

THOMPSON, SERGEANT GLEN, U.S. Army, 25th Infantry Div., 14th Infantry Regiment, Company H (Weapons). Interviewed October 23, 2001, Garland, Texas.

Glen drew his first breaths in a remote ranch home on the outskirts of Tatum, New Mexico. The building had been constructed a couple of generations earlier by his grandfather. Cows were the business of the adult Thompsons at that time, and they had several sections to pamper them on. However their problem narrowed down to the fact that in that part of the state a careful person could only run about eight head to the section. A person not so careful might likely lose everything he released on that dry range.

Glen said, "One year Daddy's total income was forty dollars. Soon we moved to the oil patch down at Monument, New Mexico. I graduated there in 1950 and came to college at T.C.U. in Fort Worth that fall.

"I wasn't doing too good in school by 1952 and decided to try the air force. Their enlistment period at that time was four years so I changed to the army for only three. I landed at Inchon in the spring of 1953. After basic training at Camp Roberts, California, I volunteered for advanced weapons training. I thought I'd put off Korea as long as possible," Glen said. "Wrong, the rest of the outfit went to Germany. Those of us in weapons school all went to Korea. Before going, I learned machine guns from one end to the other."

After the war Glen married Bobbie Taylor from Mount Pleasant, Texas. They exchanged their vows in June of 1959 and have made their home in the Dallas area since that time. Today they live in Garland, Texas.

WASHINGTON, SERGEANT JOHN M., U.S. Army, A Battery, 548th Battalion, 25th Armored Division. Interviewed October 24, 2001, Arlington, Texas.

Washington was born in Moreauville, Louisiana, on March 21, 1931. His family moved to Port Arthur where his father worked for an oil company. After graduation from high school in 1951, John attended Bishop College in Marshall, Texas. Unsure of his future career, his interest wavered, torn between the ministry and education.

In October of 1952 his country's immediate needs took precedence over his decision concerning a course of study.

After his training in the U.S., the navy's USS *Marine Lynch* delivered him safely to the harbor of Inchon, Korea, in February of 1953. Somewhere along the front the third M4A3 tank in the 35th Tank Co. waited. It had his name on it as driver, and he and the other four members of the crew had as a mission the support of the 89th Infantry. In addition they offered a little extra firepower for a group of Turks battling near them.

"We were referred to as a 'bastard outfit' with the mission of hitting the enemy then move out and disappear to return and hit him in another spot. An army tank at that time had a crew of five: commander, driver, BOG or assistant driver, loader, and a gunner."

In 1955 John married Shirley Barton. At the time she was a freshman at Bishop College. They raised two daughters, Libby and Lelo.

In August of 1957 be began a career of teaching at Carver Elementary in Port Arthur, Texas. He served a number of years at Woodrow Wilson Jr. High as a counselor before becoming a principal. Today, in retirement at Mansfield, Texas, John serves on the school board. He speaks of former students with sincere affection and pride. His support of their development and achievements is apparent. Given the chance, he likes to mention an ongoing friendship resulting from pro football coach Jimmy Johnson's days in his schools at Port Arthur.

John Washington
Photo courtesy of John Washington

Wilkinson, Cpl. Kenneth L., 1st Provisional Marine Brigade, Engineers, A Co. Interviewed September 28, 2001, Carrolton, Texas.

Wilkinson was born January 25, 1930, in Dallas, Texas. In 1947 he and other friends decided the marines offered more excitement than high school. Kenneth, a junior at the time, acted on the decision.

An old saying among servicemen of WW II and the Korean War era pertained to one's qualifications for being regarded as a seasoned veteran. Generally the comment went something like "How was it in Guam before the war?"

Using that criterion for experience, Kenneth passes muster for the Korean War. By the time it started in June of 1950, he could give a firsthand answer concerning life in Guam. His outfit had just returned to Camp Pendleton, California, when the North Koreans crossed the 38th parallel. Soon he and his marine buddies were en route back across the Pacific. His company arrived at the Port of Pusan, South Korea, August 3, 1950.

Cpl. Wilkinson fought in South Korea along the Pusan perimeter and the Naktong River before being pulled out for the invasion of Inchon on September 15. The names of landmarks and towns where he fought sometime slip past his memory, but Inchon and Seoul remain fresh in his thoughts.

November of 1950 found him miles inland beyond Seoul engaged in battle. Walking ahead of a tank looking for mines was his mission when his war ended. A burst of fire from a North Korean burp gun rendered him unconscious. He relied on details from buddies to explain what hit him.

It was his second and final battle injury. His two Purple Hearts today share space with other battle ribbons and medals in a modest display in his living room. He pointed them out with pride, but he chose to not list them in detail.

Cpl. Wilkinson married Juanita Graham on New Year's Eve, 1951. They raised three children, two boys and a girl, and today live in Carrolton, Texas.

ZELLERS, LARRY. POW during the Korean War and later U.S. Air Force chaplain. Interviewed May 8, 2001, Weatherford, Texas.

Born November 30, 1922, Larry Zellers devotes his life to bettering conditions for those around him. His first memories are of a small farming community called Hood, Texas, that is located about equal distance between Abilene and Wichita Falls.

Larry's parents moved to Weatherford when he reached ten years of age. After high school graduation he attended Weatherford Junior College before going into military service in 1942. During World War II Zellers served in the U.S. Army Air Force as an aircraft crewman operating out of England. His specialty during the war was radar. At war's end Larry planned for a lifetime of Christian service.

His interest and aptitude in electronics now occupied a priority notch below his religious calling. He entered North Texas State Teachers College. He graduated with a Bachelor of Arts degree. From North Texas Larry moved down the road to Dallas and the Perkins School of Theology. He remained there a year before accepting a missionary assignment involving a teaching position in Japan and Korea. While attending a training seminar in New York, he met a young lady named Francis. Both were assigned to teaching positions in Kaesong, Korea. Love blossomed and bound them to a life as husband and wife. They were married in Korea in 1949.

Imprisoned by the North Koreans four days after they crossed the 38th parallel in June 1950, Zellers soon learned that, "Death has an odor and a taste." In his excellent book *In Enemy Hands*, he describes it as "a pungent odor like that of scorched hair with a strong chemical taste."

Larry survived as a POW with other civilian and military personnel representing a number of nationalities. Their route from camp to camp was marked with bodies. Death without graves was too common in a land where the soil froze solid and the captors provided no tools. Still, Larry and other ministers of faith struggled mightily to provide for the sick and dying, sometimes weakening themselves beyond recovery in the process.

Helping to sustain Larry in prison was the knowledge that his wife had been evacuated to Japan. Medical needs had placed her in Seoul on the fateful day of the invasion. He was reunited with her after being released April 30, 1953, with other civilian prisoners. Their route to freedom led through China then Moscow, Russia, and on May 12, 1953, he set foot in the "land of the living in West Berlin." Larry credits the communists' desire to avoid the world press as the reason for their backdoor exit.

After his years in prison, Larry Zellers graduated in 1956 with a Masters of Divinity degree from Drew University in Madison, New Jersey. He accepted a commission as chaplain in the United States Air Force and retired in 1975. Today he and Francis enjoy life together in Weatherford, Texas.

Mr. Zeller's words, both printed and in person, are a comfort and support. His prayerful insight aids in sorting the tangled threads of confusion spun by war's disorder, aging memory, and uncertain emotions.

Postscript

Contacts with old buddies and new friends involved in the long-ago Korean conflict strengthen my belief that their effort will, in fact, forever be remembered. Doubts concerning today's generation being so involved in their own agenda as to be disinterested in events of their father's and grandfather's war are, in my judgment, unfounded. For me, this work has strengthened the most blessed of truths—that the offspring of those great men and women referred to by some as the "Greatest Generation" proved themselves in their father's image then spawned descendents equally as brave.

It is particularly rewarding to discover that the fighting men and women of the Korean War not only met their own challenge, but in its aftermath stocked this nation with later generations ready to answer their nation's call. I refer to recent events in New York; events that portray the courageous images of young officers, men and women, firemen and civilians, proving again that the torch has passed. Our nation is in good hands.

Other References

(Alphabetical listing of individuals from reference sources followed by text bibliography)

Capt. Troy Gordon Cope, MIA
> Flick, David, "Piece of the Puzzle," *The Dallas Morning News*, June 26, 2001, Page 15A.

Ernest Hemingway
> Hemingway, Ernest, *A Farewell to Arms*, Simon & Schuster, New York, NY, 1995.

(Korean War Project)
> Hal & Ted Barker (a nonprofit Web site) (www.koreanwar.org)

William K. Mackey
> March, Allison E. and McElfresh, Donald C., *Submarine or Phantom Target?*, Edisto Press, Silver Spring, Maryland, 1998.

Bill Mann
> Murdock, Mackey, *Last of the Old-Time Texans*, Republic of Texas Press, Plano, Texas, 2001.

Charles M. Russell
> Russell, Charles M., *Trails Plowed Under*, Doubleday & Company, Inc., Garden City, New York, 1927.

Larry Zellers
> Zellers, Larry, *In Enemy Hands*, Lexington: University Press of Kentucky, 1991.

George Zonge
> Tomedi, Rudy, *No Bugles, No Drums*, John Wiley & Sons, Inc., New York, NY, 1993.

Index

TMB3 586-7
LOTX